STARTING POINT
YOUR JOURNEY TO A BETTER LIFE STARTS HERE...

To my grandfather, Jack Marsden, God rest his soul – the greatest man I ever got the pleasure of knowing, my main source of motivation, the one who loved everybody and made everyone smile, the most selfless and humble soul who could spread joy in his darkest times, the one who I had the honor of being named after, and who called me his pal.
I will carry on your legacy of greatness and kindness, and make this world a better place.
I will make you proud, Grandpa.

In Loving Memory of
John F. "Jack" Marsden (aka Johnny Wonderful)
(October 1, 1932 – October 11, 2000)

STARTING POINT

Your Journey To A Better Life Starts Here...

Jack Travis

This book is not intended to replace any medical or psychological treatments for addictions or mental health issues: there is no substitute for the diagnoses, knowledge, and experience from professionals in the fields of medicine and psychology. However, my hope is that this book will help complement the professional treatments you receive in order to achieve optimal health and happiness in life.

Copyright © 2017 by John P. Travis

All rights reserved. This book or any portion of it
may not be reproduced or used in any manner whatsoever
without the express written permission of the author.

Printed in the United States of America

ISBN 978-0-692-95524-6

J. Wonderful Publishing

Author Photoshoot done by: Paul Oliver Photography

www.iamjacktravis.com

Table of Contents

Preface   *i*

Part I: The Way Things Are And Why

Chapter 1:	*The Way We Are*	*1*
Chapter 2:	*Chain Reactions*	*5*
Chapter 3:	*Understanding One Another Logically & Biologically*	*11*
Chapter 4:	*Warped Perception*	*19*
Chapter 5:	*My Layers of Knowledge Theory*	*23*
Chapter 6:	*Intelligence Can Override Aggression*	*31*
Chapter 7:	*Perceived Reality vs. Actual Reality*	*39*
Chapter 8:	*Things We Can And Cannot Control*	*43*

Part II: What We Can Do To Make A Positive Change

Chapter 9:	*The Next Phase In Our Journey*	*53*
Chapter 10:	*Time To Get Motivated!*	*57*
Chapter 11:	*Reach Out For Help!*	*59*
Chapter 12:	*Do An Overall Analysis Of Your Life*	*69*
Chapter 13:	*Start Engaging In Activities That Are Positive & Fun*	*85*
Chapter 14:	*Find Ways To Spread Positive Energy*	*89*
Chapter 15:	*Build Your Career & Your Self-Esteem*	*93*
Chapter 16:	*The Power Of Forgiveness*	*109*
Chapter 17:	*Maintaining A Balanced Life*	*113*

Acknowledgements   *iii*

Preface

Hi! My name is Jack. It's nice to meet you! You're probably wondering how a young guy like me could already know so much about life. Well, the truth is, I'm not a professional. I am simply just a guy who was down on his luck for many years and suffered through some major hardships that might be similar to yours, but through those hardships, I've gained a lot of insight and knowledge. My entire life, I have dealt with all kinds of abuse and neglect, battled a series of mental illnesses, and lived in fear. I suffered in silence, and spent lots of time feeling like I was worthless and unloved because of the way most people treated me. Because of this, I was completely destroyed as a person in almost every way possible, and I tried all kinds of different methods to fix myself; some worked and some didn't.

However, after about twenty years of darkness, I have found the light, and I am on a journey towards that light. It is the light of happiness and success in life, and I invite you and anyone you may know to join me on this magnificent journey, as we are stronger together.

The journey through life is quite an interesting one; a rather bumpy road in the beginning that may lead to either darker and bumpier roads, or a very broad and bright horizon where anything is possible. It all depends on the path you choose and the choices you make. Through our struggles, we have the potential to live and learn. Many people say that life is hard, life is stressful, or life just sucks, but the truth is life is what you make it. Your hardships will either make you or break you. It's all up to you. Just know that no matter what cards you're dealt in life, you can always use what you have to find the winning strategy.

Our struggles in life can help make us stronger and smarter as we work through them; they can even lead us to more positive outcomes. Although I had major struggles, they lead me to some amazing people who have shared some incredible wisdom. Many of these people were friends, teachers, professors, mentors, therapists, and other experts. Based on what I've learned from these wise individuals, I spent years being open-minded and trying new things, trying to figure out why I wasn't healing properly, even trying things I never thought I'd ever try before. After years of self-loathing, suicide attempts, failed relationships, binge-drinking, and being stuck in places where I didn't want to be, things started to change for me. I began seeking professional help, confronting my demons, spending time in psychiatric hospitals, attending partial hospital programs, working with different experts, trial and error experiments, and ultimately, figuring a lot of it out on my own.

My mission is to make your life easier, by sharing what I've learned, along with my many theories, techniques, and my step-by-step methods that have worked for me, and can work for you too. I have a vision of a better, safer, and more positive society where struggles are only temporary; we can't avoid struggles altogether, but we can learn to work through them early on to get to where we want to be in life. I'm not looking to create weaker human beings; I'm looking to put emphasis on the strength in numbers aspect to strengthen communities and society as a whole. If we all learned to come together and help each other, don't you think the world would be a much better place?

Unfortunately, I cannot do it alone; I'm going to need your help, and the help of as many people as possible. Help me help you, and help society. We can all make a difference if we collaborate. Are you willing to do whatever it takes to build the life you want and deserve? Well, if you already picked up my book and started reading, you're off to a great start! Now, let me guide you on the adventure ahead, as I welcome you on my journey to true happiness and success in life. We're thrilled to have you. Follow me!

PART I

THE WAY THINGS ARE AND WHY

If you find this book helpful to you,
Please refer it to a loved one in need...

Chapter 1

The Way We Are

Hi! Thank for you joining me on my journey! There is much to explore! The best place to start is discussing how society currently is. The world we live in today is quite an interesting one, and although it has shown great improvements over the years, it still has its imperfections. We still see lots of sadness and negativity in the world, from unhappiness to mental illness, or even to people committing crimes and murdering each other. Many people can't even get through a whole day without smoking a pack of cigarettes, drinking a handle of liquor, or doing worse things to themselves and others. The world can be a scary place, and this can lead to many people being misunderstood. These kinds of negative behaviors are not inherited, nor do they originate from one person. Instead, they are learned and passed down by the generations before them.

The problem is, not everybody knows how to deal with personal issues properly. We often encounter different people who are just so unhappy no matter what, and no good things in life ever change that. Of course, there are people who turn to lives of crime, people who are clinically depressed and spending time in the hospital, or even people who just live a sad lonely life and don't fulfill what they truly want to. There are many people out there like that, but what about the ones who do land good jobs, make great money, get married, have kids, and even have friends and coworkers all around them, yet for some reason they are still not happy? There are even people out there who win the lottery and don't have to work, but often report being really depressed a year later.

We often do our best to get through life, but what happens when the people closest to us are the ones hurting us or turning their backs on us? Unfortunately, no matter what we go through, certain people just won't understand. Not everybody has high levels of intelligence or understanding, and they often take things personally, or simply just don't want to deal with other people's problems. Many of us don't realize how much that can truly hurt someone, and we are not always aware of the consequences. One thing I noticed my whole life was that many of the things I've done to others were done to me later on by someone else. In some way, shape, or form, I believe that I felt how I made others feel at certain times. This refers to the law of reaping and sowing, which basically states that the seeds we plant eventually become the crops we harvest. However, most people are more familiar with karma; stemming from Hinduism and Buddhism, it states that doing good brings good things, and doing bad brings bad things. I noticed it in other people too; I've seen people who hurt me get hurt themselves in a similar way, or people who hurt others get hurt in a similar way as well. I witnessed the same thing for those who helped others, including myself; we would get rewarded for our good behavior in some way.

What does it take to find true happiness and success in life? Can I ever find true happiness after all I've been through? Do I even deserve to be happy? Why am I even here?

These are questions many people may commonly ask themselves or others. Many feel lost in life, or that they have predetermined fates or destinies that they can't avoid. The truth is, our fates or destinies are not predetermined, in fact, they are shaped by our daily actions and decisions. Suicide was almost my fate; I spent many nights trying to end my life with many different strategies, but instead of being six feet under, I made a choice to stay alive, and I took action. I got the help I needed, and I did whatever I had to do to get to where I am now, and where I will be in the future. Anybody can turn their lives around; in order to be unlimited, we must remove the limits we set for ourselves.

The world we live in will not change if we do nothing but hope for change; in order for improvements to occur, action must be taken. It will take more than just one person to influence change; it will take the help of as many people as possible. We must start movements to create better societal norms. Society has shown amazing improvements in the last century, and even in the last forty to fifty years; we've seen both the light and dark sides of humanity throughout history. Although we have achieved amazing things beyond what any of us could have ever imagined, we have also done horrible things and displayed destructive and aggressive behavior that devastated and traumatized many people. Once we all choose to learn from the negative and move towards the positive, we can make great things happen. The best place to start is with ourselves; we must learn from the mistakes others have made to harm us, and choose to do better. In other words, we must break the negative chain reactions and start positive ones.

Chapter 2

Chain Reactions

It is important to understand exactly why people do bad things to others, and that their behavior does not originate from them. When people behave certain ways, it is because they learn it from the people they are surrounded by the most; whether they are their parents, siblings, relatives, friends, neighbors, communities, etc. People who grow up in unhealthy, negative households typically display more aggressive behavior and feel less empathy and sympathy for others; what their parents don't realize is that they primed them to be self-destructive. Their negative behavior towards others makes others not like them, and they don't end up getting the social support and guidance they need to live a truly happy life. Though there are cases where some people will try to help those who are disadvantaged, but they end up getting badly hurt themselves. We need to understand that abuse is a cycle, and many refer to such phenomena as either the domino effect or the ripple effect, but I prefer the term *chain reaction*.

A *chain reaction* is defined as a series of events, which are typically caused by the previous ones. Many chain reactions in life are negative ones, and there are many examples of those. For instance, let's look at the life of an innocent young boy who is abused and neglected at home by both parents, he's bullied at school, and nobody helps him or sticks up for him. As time goes on, he feels disconnected because he's not getting the support he needs from others, so he starts having dark fantasies and shows signs of becoming a sociopath. Since he acts strangely, most people avoid him and ridicule him, making him feel worse. Then, one day, he finally snaps, brings a gun to school, and starts shooting people; he kills about twenty people. Next thing you know, he ruins his life, he's hated even more by everyone and looked at as a monster, and he's serving a life sentence in prison. Surrounded by other criminals, felons, and murderers, he gets ganged up on in prison worse than he did in his old life outside of prison. Sadly, he can't take the societal rejection anymore, and he hangs himself in his prison cell. Sadly, things like this happen all the time. In fact, we see it on the news every once in awhile. Most people who shoot up schools are looked at as monsters, but in reality, they are misunderstood victims who never got help.

Here's a more common and slightly less scary example; a man works hard to provide for his family, but he hates his job. The truth is, he does not get fair raises, he has not had any promotions, people who started much later than he did get promoted sooner, and his boss constantly ridicules him and yells at him. It does not end there; the man comes home every night stressed out, and hating his life. He drinks, he smokes, and worst of all, he yells at his wife and children and gets angry over little things, which makes them feel like they are always walking on eggshells in their own home. The problems in the marriage cause his wife to begin drinking to cope with stress, and when he's at work and the kids are home, she screams at them constantly over little things, and puts them down all the time. Their kids have a rough life at home, and when they go to school, they bully other kids. Unfortunately, those poor kids getting bullied resort to drug use and self-harm, and one of them ends up overdosing later that year.

These scenarios are quite scary and devastating, but they can be prevented. What we need to understand from them is that our actions and experiences affect more than just ourselves; they affect everyone around us in some way. Not everyone knows how to control their actions, but it is possible for anyone to learn. One of the best things anyone can do to discontinue these negative chain reactions is to properly learn how to deal with anger. Anger is what I call a very ugly emotion, and even though it is necessary for our survival, it can pose a major threat as well. Abuse is born from anger; when people get angry with others, they often abuse them by saying or doing hurtful things. This can have devastating effects on the victims, which continues those negative chain reactions. I would like to share a technique with you that I have developed for dealing with anger. I have used it myself and it works great. The next time someone makes you angry, and you think about saying or doing something to hurt them, here's what you need to do:

How To Deal With Anger Properly
Step 1
Take a step back from the situation.
Step 2
Take A Deep Breath
Step 3
Ask Yourself, "Will I Regret This Later?"
Step 4
If yes, remove yourself from the situation, and find a healthy way to cope and physically exert the anger. *(Any form of exercise is recommended)*
Step 5
Come back with a calm, clear mind and readdress the situation to resolve it.

This technique is effective because it allows you to deal with your intense emotions rationally without hurting anyone, and you can then solve the situation properly with a rational thought process. I'm sure many of us have regretted the things we have said to people when we were angry; I know I certainly have. By effectively dealing with negative emotions, we no longer add to the problem and burden ourselves with more guilt and shame. Instead, we take back control, and solve the problem at hand. In order to prevent us from getting angry again over the same situation, we must resolve the situation properly.

Much like preventative tactics, we can also discontinue a negative chain reaction by starting a new positive one. Take this one, for instance. A guy has a long day at work, and he looks forward to coming home and spending some quality time with his girlfriend, who he loves dearly. He even surprises her with flowers, but comes home to a big surprise himself; he catches his girlfriend in bed with his best friend. Totally shocked and distraught, he freezes and doesn't know what to do, and then, with a moment of insanity, he kicks them both out and has a meltdown. He could have killed them both if he wanted to, but he chose not to, instead, he chose to do positive things. Of course he feels certain emotions such as sadness, anger, surprise, heartbreak, etc., but he deals with them properly. He starts engaging in healthy coping mechanisms such as running, splitting wood, hitting the punching bag, listening to music, meditating, and even talking to close friends and family. He decides to look at this as an opportunity to reinvent himself, so he starts going to the gym regularly, speaking with a therapist, helping his community, and engaging in fun activities to meet better friends. After awhile, he ends up getting in really great shape, and he chases his dreams once he learns more about himself. As years go by, he becomes a much stronger, smarter, and more successful person, and he learns to forgive his ex-girlfriend and ex-best friend. Not only that, but he thanks them for giving him the motivation and the opportunity to become the person he is today.

The person in this example is a great role model for others; turning a negative into a positive to benefit himself and prevent him from hurting others. If more people could learn how to do this, we would start having less of these issues persist. It may be a lot easier said than done, I know from experience, but the truth is, it all starts with a decision. The decision

Chain Reactions

you need to make is whether or not to let a certain experience make you or break you. You must be strong enough and smart enough to know yourself well enough or the person you truly want to be well enough. When others hurt you, no matter how angry they might make you, or whether or not you begin having dark revenge fantasies, you need to deal with those intense negative emotions properly by using my technique, or any other technique that works best for you, and remind yourself that you are a better person than they are and that you will not let this bump in the road ruin the rest of your journey.

A crucial thing we must all understand about abusers is that they do not always realize what they are doing; they often perceive it as normal, depending on how they grew up and what they have learned in life. We must not only stay out of abusive situations, but also try to sympathize with our abusers on a healthy level and forgive them; that way, we do not turn around and abuse them back. After all, our parents always taught us that two wrongs don't make a right. Before you go bashing someone who hurt you in life, take a moment to think about how it feels when you hurt someone, feel guilty for it, and feel even worse when they refuse to forgive you and bash you down. Every perpetrator was once a victim, so don't continue to hurt them like others did because that is wrong. Sweet revenge will always turn sour no matter what, so we need to learn to forgive and sympathize, and maybe even empathize because you know how it feels to be abused. Trust me, I used to have problems forgiving people, and I would hold grudges for years; little did I realize I was only hurting myself by focusing on the negative. The main factor that helped me learn to forgive was understanding people not as individuals who hurt me, but as a whole species of animals on both a logical and a biological level.

Chapter 3

Understanding One Another Logically and Biologically

One of the main reasons why there is so much conflict and hatred in the world is simply because there is a lack of understanding among most individuals. Many people simply just believe that some people are bad and some people are good. These biases blind us from seeing the bigger picture. The truth is, nobody is just bad and nobody is just good; we all have the potential to be both, so we're not that different from one another. In fact, modern science has proved that everybody's DNA is about 99.9% similar, which goes to show that genetically, we're all almost exactly alike. We do have very slight differences such as ethnicities, certain physical characteristics, opposite genders, etc., but we all function exactly the same. The only big differences among individuals are personal experiences because nobody has the exact same experiences or perspectives as anyone else. In order to fully understand others and ourselves and set aside conflicts and hatred, we must understand humans, as animals, on both a logical and a biological level.

IT IS ALL ABOUT SURVIVAL

The first thing you must realize is that even though we are an advanced and intelligent species, we are still animals, and living organisms. We often see the many things that different people and animals do and the way they act in certain situations, and many of us wonder why they act those ways. The truth is, every action a person or animal takes and every decision they make is meant to ensure their survival. Essentially, we are all built and designed to survive.

Basically, in the animal kingdom, there are two main types of survival; there's one's own survival and survival of the whole species. Many species of animals, and even plants and other organisms, depend on each other for survival simply because there are certain tasks that are too much for one to take on. You know what they say, strength in numbers. Naturally, every species, even humans, will look out for both the survival of themselves and other members of the species. When we look at the environment and the planet as a whole, we see that every species has a niche, or makes an important contribution to the planet. For example, different animals in the food chain (prey and predators) control each other's populations, plants and animals exchange oxygen and carbon dioxide, animal waste fertilizes plants, producers feed herbivorous consumers, and of course the microorganisms that decompose decaying matter and live inside us all; without them, we wouldn't be able to function. As you can see, all species of organisms really do work together to keep our planet fertile, sustainable, and inhabitable. This is the reason why we have empathy and sympathy, so we instinctually know to help one another to survive. After all, we each play an important role to the planet's overall health.

On the flip side, there are situations where we really do need to look out for ourselves; when there is an immediate threat to our survival, our fight or flight responses kick in. Our fight or flight responses are capable of having our bodies do many amazing things such as dilating our pupils to see better, heightening all of our senses, pumping our bodies full of adrenaline and glucose, blood flowing to our skeletal muscles to increase our physical strength, the universal biochemical energy molecule, ATP (adenosine tri-phosphate), being released from our muscles and giving us sudden bursts of energy, and yes, you guessed it, temporarily disabling our ability to feel empathy and sympathy. That's right, when our fight or flight responses kick in, and the choice is survive or die, we no longer feel empathy or sympathy for the time being; the main reason for this is because if we're being attacked by someone, and we do feel empathy or sympathy for them, they would have a competitive advantage and most likely kill us because we'll hesitate to fight back. It's wonderful to look out for others, but your life is just as important as theirs, which is why it's good to trust your animal instincts if someone else doesn't care very much about your well being. When it comes down to it, the more one has to compete for survival, the more aggressive one will become.

INTELLIGENCE IS KEY

Luckily, us humans have the biggest competitive advantage in the animal kingdom. We may not be the strongest, the fastest, the largest, or the most agile, but we are the smartest. Our advanced intelligence has allowed us to do amazing things and make our way to the top of the food chain. If you take a look back at history, we were hunter/gatherers for thousands of years, and then things changed when we discovered how to plant seeds and control plant growth, which led us to developing agriculture. The development of agriculture allowed us to have food surpluses, which limited the needs to spend time hunting and gathering, thus allowing us to adapt to be less aggressive and competitive since we no longer needed to be all the time. As the first civilizations formed, so did the first governments, and the first laws and regulations were created to help control ourselves. This led to societies and the development of new societal norms.

The key factor to creating societal norms is the idea of mob mentality, or the idea that humans, and other animals, will copy what they see others do. For example, if one person drops to the ground, or "hits the deck", it is very likely that other people around them will too. There are two main reasons why this phenomenon naturally occurs without thinking about it; either we assume that there's an immediate danger that others are aware of and we aren't, or because we subconsciously know that mimicking the people around us will allow us to be accepted by them. Like I said previously, we depend on one another for survival, so if we see someone performing a certain action such as running away from something, hitting the deck, screaming, or responding to environmental stimuli in any way, our brains automatically assume that they have an awareness of danger that we don't, which makes us copy what they do, assuming it is what we need to do to survive. In addition to that, we have a natural tendency to adapt to the people we're surrounded with most in order to be more like them. If we act differently, people could either reject us or attack us, which would be a threat to our survival. Since loneliness can lead to depression and we need positive social bonds to survive, we do whatever we need to do to be socially accepted in order to optimize our chances of survival.

HUMANS MAKE THINGS COMPLICATED

In the modern day human world, things have become more structured and organized, but also a lot more complicated. We have our two types of survival; one's own survival and survival of the whole species, but in the human world, each of them have two subdivisions; biological survival and economic survival. Biological survival is simply sustaining life or staying alive; this involves activities such as eating food, drinking water, breathing, staying healthy, showing aggression when necessary, and reproducing to create future life. Economic survival, on the other hand, has to do with having enough money to cover your costs of living; which includes working a job, paying bills, being of a good socio-economic status, medical expenses, extra spending money for leisure activities, etc. These two subdivisions happen to be intertwined, because in the modern world, we need money to be able to afford the things we need to sustain life.

Understanding One Another Logically & Biologically

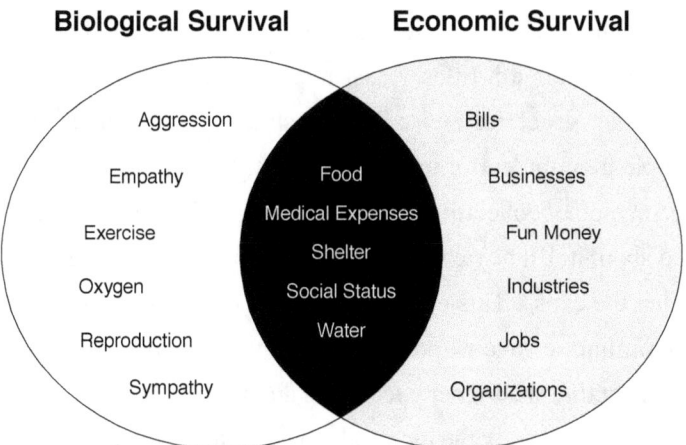

You may have heard many people say that money is "the root of all evil," well the truth is that we all need money to survive in today's world. Let's face it, almost everything costs money now days, and the reason for that is simple; resources are limited and supply and demand must balance each other out. In the world of business, anyone who charges you money has to pay money first. For instance, restaurants charge people money to eat there because they have to pay for their food, their bills, and their employees, the facilities and distributors that sell them food products buy the raw resources from farmers and they have to pay employees plus cover their manufacturing overhead, and then farmers have their bills and mortgages to pay as well. The overall economy works like a circular flow with many layers, which makes everyone need to pay their dues.

Socio-economic status can play a role in one's overall mental health and survival for many reasons. For example, self-esteem can play a huge role in someone's socio-economic status because people with low self-esteem often suffer from abuse and neglect, which makes them feel unworthy and unwanted. Often times, they may lack the guidance or discipline to do good in school or even go to college, which only makes things worse. Now days, the costs of living are so high that minimum-wage is not enough to cover them unless you work a ridiculous amount of hours, plus the workers may feel less important because others look down on them and their job titles. Trust me, I learned this from experience; I used to bag groceries and collect trash at a supermarket for 6 years, and people thought less of me because of it. In fact, one time a customer insulted my job of collecting trash to my face, and when I told her, "I'm not worried about it, I'll be rich someday." she replied with, "Yeah, if you start collecting the cans." This experience taught me to better myself and also to treat minimum wage workers with the upmost respect they deserve, the same respect that the higher executives and CEOs get, because minimum wage workers are really the most valuable workers to a company. After all, they're the one's generating all of the revenue; taking customers orders, stocking shelves with products, preparing food, driving delivery vehicles, etc. Without them, there would be very few companies.

Since the costs of living are so high, there are many people who end up stuck in unhealthy living situations simply because they cannot afford to live anywhere else. Examples of unhealthy living situations are having abusive or neglectful parents, domestic violence, unhealthy relationships, substance abuse, household conflicts, being too crowded, being alone, homelessness, etc. Usually, children, teenagers, and young adults have it the worst when it comes to unhealthy living situations, especially because of the lack of control at an early age, and not having a way out. There are also many college students who have to go to classes, do homework, take exams, and work a minimum wage job on top of that to try to get ahead and stay ahead. When they're abused at home or told they're not good enough or trying hard enough, it really hurts them because they're just doing their best to get to the next stage in life. They really don't need the added stress and pressures from family members.

Of course, in the animal kingdom, when animals are mistreated by their families or others, they can simply just leave and form their own social groups, but in the human world, it's not that simple because we are limited by our income and required to abide by certain societal norms, such as living in a home and not on the streets. This is why people tend to develop these mental illnesses because they are constantly being harmed or threatened in some way. The important thing to understand about the human body is that it has evolved to constantly heal, regenerate, and balance itself out. We're constantly adapting to our surrounding environments in order to survive. If we're not healing from something, mental or physical, or even emotional, it means that we're being affected by external factors. We constantly respond certain ways to different environmental stimuli in order to survive because environmental stressors trigger our fight or flight responses and can cause our brain chemistry to become imbalanced, but once we are away from the certain danger, our brain chemistry will balance itself out, after some time away, to put us back into a healthy or stable mental state.

If we are constantly exposed to environmental stressors, like being in unhealthy living situations, we adapt to survive by becoming more aggressive and constantly on edge and high alert. It's very important to understand that when someone suffers from a mental illness, genetics plays a very small role, and external or environmental factors play the biggest role. Think about it this way, what happens when you don't treat an infection or when you pick at a scab? You guessed it! You don't heal properly.

Not only do mentally ill people have a lot of harmful environmental factors contributing to their illnesses, but they also may not entirely have what they need to get better. When you think about it, with an infection that you can't recover from on your own, you will need some outside help from antibiotics and Vitamin C; kind of the same idea with treating a mental illness. When it comes down to it, the absolute basic elements we need to optimize our survival are food, water, oxygen, sunlight, shelter, and positive social bonds. Food, water, and oxygen are vital to sustain life, sunlight gives us vitamin D, shelters offer us protection, and of course, positive social bonds offer us more protection and help; thus giving us a greater chance of survival.

Therefore, in order to heal, we need more good in our lives. Mental illnesses or unhappiness tend to persist when a person has too much bad, not enough good, or a combination of both in their lives. The key is to begin eliminating the bad and start finding the good, which I will explain how to do later on. Getting the support you need to heal may be difficult at first, but once you learn the right resources to start with, it makes the healing process quicker and easier.

Chapter 4

Warped Perception

Now that you understand the basics of survival instincts and how we work on a biological level, it's time to go a little more in depth with it. Like I said before, even though we're 99.9% similar genetically, our experiences differ. Our survival mechanisms all work the same, but how we learn and adapt totally depends on our immediate environmental stimuli. This leads to the idea of people having a *warped perception*, or the idea that we all perceive things differently based on our unique life experiences. A good example of this is seen in victims of abuse; if a woman is abused by enough men in her life, she may perceive all men as a threat to her survival, or vice versa. The reason why this occurs is because our brains will subconsciously make automatic assumptions based on negative past experiences. We have the ability to identify and analyze significant characteristics of the people, animals, etc. who hurt us in anyway, and apply those to everyday life. When we encounter different people, animals, etc. with similar attributes, we tend to avoid them because our survival instincts tell us that they are a threat to our survival, even if they are not in actuality.

A great example of this in my life has to do with my first school experience. When I was 3 years old, I started preschool where I was badly abused by my teacher. I won't get too much into detail, but what she did severely traumatized me for most of my childhood. Since that was my first experience with a teacher, my brain made the automatic assumption that all teachers and authority figures were a threat to my survival, and that I should avoid them in the future. This lead to many issues such as being too afraid to ask teachers for help when I needed it, not getting the grades I could've gotten, and not being able to develop close relationships with them. I also never fought back when bullies made fun of me or attacked me physically because I was too scared that if I did, the teachers would beat me even harder, and I would get in even more trouble at home. Although that would've been an unlikely outcome, it was how I perceived it because of my past experiences.

Another good example is when you eat or drink something that makes you sick. I'm sure we've all had those times when we got food poisoning or had a little too much to drink, I'm sure you probably either said, "I'm never eating there again!" or "I'm never going to drink ever again!" with your face in the toilet and people holding your hair back. When that happens, you often feel nauseous from the look, the smell, or even just the thought of that specific food or alcoholic beverage, am I right? The reason for that is because your brain automatically assumes that those foods or beverages will always make you sick and to never eat or drink them again. Remember that vomiting is a bodily reflex for expelling toxins in the stomach, so you're brain will subconsciously perceive anything that makes you puke as a harmful toxin. Even though the real truth is that not all of those foods are bad, or that alcohol is okay in moderation, your warped perception will make you think otherwise.

It's important to know that the reason why our perceptions get warped is because we adapt to our immediate experiences in life to ensure our survival; we constantly learn from our struggles and our mistakes to improve ourselves for a greater chance at survival. All of our experiences in life are unique yet similar, but we are all affected by them the same way. Some are affected more than others because naturally we all have different tolerance levels. We need to be considerate of people's different tolerance levels and try our best to understand what they've been through and how it may have affected them. Even though our experiences differ and some are worse than others, people who haven't quite had it "as bad" as someone else don't know any worse. This is referred to as what I call a unique worst experience.

For instance, let's assume that both Dave and Sam were abused at home growing up. Dave might say, "My mother called me names and put me down all the time when she drank." Then Sam might say, "Dude, that's nothing. My father would drink a lot after my mother left, and he'd burn me with his cigarettes and beat me with his belt." Then, he show's Dave his burn marks. Although Sam's situation seems worse, both situations can be very damaging to a person at a young age. If the worst thing that Dave experienced was his mother verbally abusing him, he does not personally know any worse. Therefore, that is his unique worst experience from his perspective. It is crucial that we understand this and make sure we don't give anyone a hard time if his or her experiences aren't as bad as ours because by doing that, we would be abusing someone who has already been abused.

The last thing we need to understand about warped perception is that it can affect our senses of right and wrong. For the most part, everyone has a sense of right and wrong, but not everyone's sense of right and wrong is exactly the same. A person's sense of right and wrong is mostly based on what they learn in life and what they grow up with; they may perceive what they are doing as right, when really it is wrong. This is why sometimes people don't feel guilty for doing something wrong because in their mind, they're doing the right thing, so they feel good about it. This can lead to conflicts and biases when other people see what they're doing and know that it's wrong; and if people don't understand why that person is doing what they are doing, they will automatically assume that that person is simply just the scum of the earth. We often see this occur in sadists or sociopaths because of their antisocial personality disorders and unique life experiences that traumatize them. When a person suffers from abuse, neglect, or trauma growing up, they are very likely to become a sociopath or a sadist. The reason why they want to hurt others is not because they're evil, it's because the majority of people in their lives have abused them, so their brains make the automatic assumption that all people are like that. With this warped mindset, their brains tell them that everyone is out to get them, and that if they want to survive, they need to eliminate everyone else by hurting or killing them. They often target people with similar characteristics to their abusers in life, which is why we see serial killers murder people who tend to have similar attributes. In the mind of a sociopath, they believe that people who look or act like their abusers are evil, and they must be eliminated if they want to survive, so they believe they are doing the right thing. In the eyes of the law, and most people, we know that what they are doing is wrong, so we either shun them or punish them.

The truth is, people who are that far-gone need to get help as soon as possible in order to clarify their perceptions and prevent them from hurting anyone. I will explain later on what people can do to get help and see the bigger picture. Basically, seeking out professional help is the proper thing to do in order to help you see things properly. If we expand our knowledge and learn the real truths, it can help us retrain our brains to think differently and break out of our unhealthy patterns.

Chapter 5

My Layers of Knowledge Theory

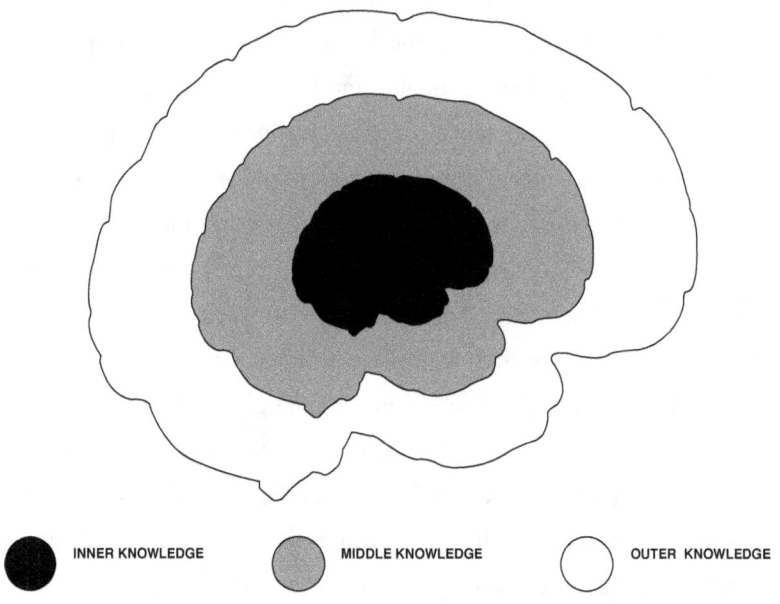

The important thing to understand about warped perception is that we are limited by our own knowledge, which develops in layers over many years of learning and experience. After a life time of abuse, neglect, and trauma, along with working with professionals, mentors, professors, teachers, etc., plus, what I figured out from personal experience and experimenting, it led me to an amazing revelation. Thus, my Layers of Knowledge Theory was created. I have discovered that all humans have three main layers of knowledge; inner knowledge, middle knowledge, and outer knowledge. Keep in mind that lease layers do not exist in the physical world, as they are intangible.

Chapter 5

INNER KNOWLEDGE

Inner knowledge is the inner most layer of knowledge that we all have, and it is the same in all of us. It is the very basic knowledge we are all born with, and it consists of all of our basic animal instincts such as hunger, thirst, breathing, senses, sleep, emotions, aggression, libido, intuition, etc. All of the instincts and functions we have as organisms that we need to ultimately survive, adapt, and reproduce. Inner knowledge is mostly involuntary, as we sense it and feel it most times without having to think about it. A prime example of that would be when we're hungry, our stomachs growl; that's our inner knowledge telling us that we need to replenish in order to sustain life. When we become sexually aroused, that is our inner knowledge encouraging us to reproduce and keep our species alive. When we feel negative emotions, our inner knowledge is telling us that something is wrong and a change needs to be made, and positive emotions tell us that we are in a healthy situation. You get the basic idea. Inner knowledge is a fixed layer that doesn't change because we are all born with it, and it is exactly the same in everyone. However, it does influence the other two layers greatly, and the other two layers can vary in structure and thickness based on personal experiences.

MIDDLE KNOWLEDGE

Middle knowledge is the knowledge gained from our responses to immediate environmental stimuli, or better known as street smarts. We learn this knowledge from the things taught to us from our parents, our families, and our overall interactions with the people around us. Remember that everyone's DNA is 99.9% similar, and the biggest differences are our experiences. Due to warped perception, we constantly adapt to our personal experiences in order to learn from them, ultimately ensuring our survival. Negative stimuli will typically respond with introverted or aggressive behavior. For example, if a kid is walking across the playground at school, and two other kids chase him down and start beating him up, he will either involuntarily choose fight, flight, or freeze depending on what he was taught early in life through his experiences. Unfortunately, because of my experience with my preschool teacher at the age of 3, I was always afraid to fight back when I was bullied because I feared the teachers punishing me and beating me even worse than the other kids. Due to my past experiences, I involuntarily chose freeze because my middle knowledge told me that was my greatest chance of survival.

Middle knowledge can also contain the social norms we learn from our families, which may not be acceptable in other places. This can cause certain groups of people to reject us because we act differently than they do. Since we all rely on social acceptance to optimize our chances of survival, we fit in with the people who are most like us because they will accept us; just as the saying goes, "birds of a feather flock together." Many people are the way that they are because of their middle knowledge, especially if they're poorly educated and lack outside perspective. Think about all of the advice given to you by people older and supposedly wiser than you, you may have followed that advice assuming that they knew the way of the world, right? Well, like I mentioned earlier, everyone is limited by their own knowledge, and not everyone knows exactly what's right and wrong or how things work. For the best advice, whatever you want to know or gain insight on, make sure to go to the experts or credible sources that you can trust.

OUTER KNOWLEDGE

Outer knowledge is the knowledge we gain from an outer perspective outside of our immediate environments and social groups. This is the knowledge we acquire from education, career training, experiences, therapy, mentorship, fellowships, books, Internet research, networking, etc. This is the most powerful knowledge, which can take years to gain, but it can even override your animal instincts and balance you out. Most of us adapt to a conformed and civilized society because it is essential for our economic survival. This goes back to the idea of mob mentality because we learn to mimic the people we're surrounded with the most in order to be socially accepted. Thanks to outer knowledge, we can slowly make paradigm shifts in order to better ourselves and advance to be what we truly want to be in life.

INTERACTIONS BETWEEN LAYERS

Like I've already stated previously, inner knowledge is fixed and will not change simply because we're all born with it and it is exactly the same for everyone. The middle and outer layers, however, can vary in structure and thickness based on our unique life experiences, but the inner layer influences them both. The middle and outer layers are dynamic, and they tend to balance each other out in direct response to immediate environmental stimuli. When it comes to balancing each other out, the thicker layer, or the dominant layer, will most likely take over in most situations whether or not they are intense.

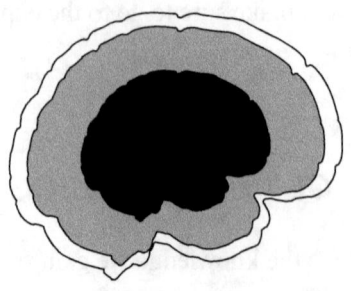

LESS INTELLIGENT, MORE AGGRESSIVE

People who are less educated are likely to have dominant middle knowledge layers because they mostly know what they've lived rather than what school or the outside world could have taught them. People like this are likely to be more aggressive in certain situations because they rely more on survival instincts influencing their middle knowledge layers; in other words, they think and act emotionally rather than logically.

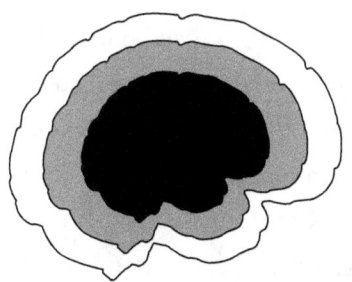

MORE INTELLIGENT, LESS AGGRESSIVE

People who are more educated outside of their immediate environments and have learned a lot from their teachers, professors, mentors, etc. develop dominant outer knowledge layers. When people become smart enough to learn how the world really works beyond their family's beliefs and reasoning, they can learn the real truths and have a clearer perception of the world around them. Depending on what and how much they learn, their outer knowledge layers will most likely override their middle knowledge layers, which will allow them to think and act logically rather than emotionally. Overall, people with dominant outer knowledge layers tend to handle situations more efficiently.

HOW THE LAYERS FORM

We all start by being born with our inner knowledge layers; they are formed during embryonic and fetal development, and as newborns, it is all we have to rely on mentally. As we start growing and learning how to survive from our parents or guardians, this is when our middle knowledge layers begin to develop. Our mothers either breast feed us or start us off on baby formula, and we learn what our food is and whom our first allies are. We naturally form special bonds with our parents because we depend on them for survival. As we grow and develop in our early years, we become curious and explore the world around us. As our bones and muscles develop, we learn how to crawl, walk, run, etc., and we also learn the things that our parents teach us, whether or not they mean to. In other words, we assume that what people around us do is what we must do to survive, which is why young children mimic what they see others do in real life or on TV.

Once it becomes time in our lives to start going to school, this is when our outer knowledge layers begin to develop. We interact with new adult authority figures and other children our own age, allowing us to develop social skills and learn things beyond what we're taught at home. The biggest game changer for us is when we learn how to read because learning how to read unlocks a whole new world of information we can absorb from books, articles, the internet, etc. As we go through school, we learn all of the basic skills we need in life, such as reading, math, and language, and the things we don't need as much but we categorize as common knowledge, like history, literature, science, etc.

The development of our outer knowledge layers depends on how we're influenced by our families and other people at school, also how much we pay attention and the amount of relevant information we retain. There are people who totally believe everything their families teach them, whether they are right or wrong, and stick to those beliefs no matter what they are taught in school. Not everyone makes it to college or even graduates high school, which can make it tough for them to expand their outer knowledge layers.

THE 70:30 RATIO

Ideally, in life, everything is all about balance; too much and not enough can be equally as bad. Everybody's outer layer to middle layer ratio is different because of our unique life experience, but through learning and therapy, we can learn to properly balance our layers out. Even though balance is key, the ideal balance between layers is not even on both sides; the ideal outer layer to middle layer thickness ratio is approximately 70:30. The reason for this is because with a dominant outer knowledge layer, you will be able to think logically rather than emotionally and handle situations that may have once baffled you. However, because of your immediate environments and past experiences, you will need to rely on your middle layer for survival in certain life-threatening situations. Luckily, having a dominant outer layer will make you smarter and more likely to avoid or be prepared for those kinds of life-threatening situations. After all, you never know when life is going to throw you a curve ball and really test you.

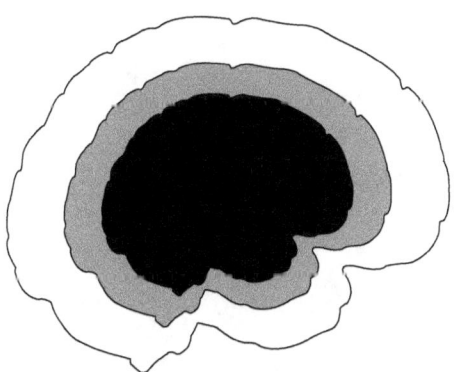

**IDEAL OUTER TO MIDDLE RATIO:
70:30**

Chapter 6

Intelligence Can Override Aggression

Now that you understand the basics of survival instincts, warped perception, and how our knowledge forms in layers, you can now understand my very basic principle in human behavior; the fact that intelligence can override aggression. Like we stated in the previous chapter, people with more dominant outer knowledge layers are more likely to react to most situations logically rather than emotionally, and people with dominant middle knowledge layers are more likely to react emotionally rather than logically in most situations. This leads back to how our most elementary form of knowledge, our inner knowledge, influences both of those layers, but we all only start off with those basic animal instincts that we all have.

So basically, much like Sigmund Freud's model of the psychic apparatus (the id, the ego, and the superego), or the traditional angel on one shoulder and devil on the other telling you what to you, we often have those internal conflicts with our societal norms/moral values and our animal instincts/urges. An important thing we all must comprehend is that everyone has the exact same animal instincts, or inner knowledge layers, but societal norms and moral values differ vastly depending on different cultures, environments, families, socio-economic statuses, etc. This creates a lot of conflicts between different people because of how we perceive things. For instance, a lower class family with weak structure who are less humble might talk openly about things such as sex, drinking, drugs, fighting, etc., and even though they perceive all of those things as normal and acceptable, people of higher class who come from well structured households with strong religious views and were raised to be modest might look at that with absolute disgust. Remember, everything is all about perception, which can often be warped based on our life experiences.

Many people think it is just as simple as some people are bad and some people are good, but the truth is, it is a bit more complex than that. Ultimately, it's not whether people are good or bad, or even whether they think more about themselves or others; that all has to do with how we, as individuals, perceive the world around us. The truth lies within our unique experiences, and whether we have dominant outer knowledge layers or dominant middle knowledge layers. It's the same difference between wild animals and domesticated animals. As a matter of fact, humans were the first domesticated animals. That's right! We have been domesticating wild animals for many centuries, but we were the first to be truly domesticated.

HUMANS WERE THE FIRST DOMESTICATED ANIMALS

Even though we have superior intellect beyond what any other species on Earth could imagine, we are still animals, which many of us tend to forget. The days of human domestication began shortly after we began to develop agriculture, which put an end to hunting and gathering. Having these food surpluses gave us more free time to build the first civilizations and form the first governments; societal norms and expectations began to transform our behavior due to the laws of mob mentality, ultimately domesticating us. We all conform to our societies and follow those norms and laws in order to fit in and be accepted by others, thus, optimizing our chance of survival and cooperating instead of competing.

Here's something to think about: why are wild animals so dangerous? The answer is simple; it's because they lack our level of intellect. Remember that humans are the only species with outer knowledge layers, and all other animals only rely on the instincts they were born with, and what they learn by responding directly to immediate environmental stimuli. In other words, the inner and middle knowledge layers. The most common fear is the fear of the unknown, and the only way to overcome that fear is by gaining knowledge. When we aren't sure whether or not something is a direct threat to our survival, our survival instincts will tell us "better safe than sorry." This "better safe than sorry" instinct, as I call it, will generate fear, thus triggering the fight or flight response. The "better safe than sorry" instinct is present in all animals, which is why when we get close to a wild animal, such as a deer or a rabbit, they will run away, or attack us if we get too close.

This same phenomenon can be seen in people with lower intelligence or socio-economic status, especially those who grew up in rough neighborhoods or broken homes. It all depends on the immediate environment a person was raised in and how others treated them. For example, if a person was raised in an environment where they were constantly abused and their personal growth and development was not properly nurtured, they are very likely to adapt to be more aggressive and less trusting of others. Unless they are willing to gain an outside perspective to change how they think, they will most likely live a very hard life and be stuck in an unhealthy pattern of thinking.

STIMULUS AND RESPONSE: WITHOUT KNOWLEDGE VERSUS WITH KNOWLEDGE

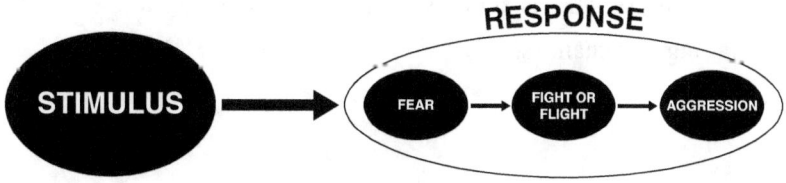

Take a look at the diagram on the previous page, which explains how stimulus and response works in most animals, including humans who are not as aware. As you can see, it all starts off with the stimulus in our environment. As I said earlier, without having the knowledge needed to handle or understand the stimulus, it will generate fear, trigger our fight or flight response, and, if necessary, cause us to display aggressive behavior. With most animals, aggressive behavior is mostly physical, and involves attacking one another and making loud noises. In humans, however, aggressive behavior often starts off with verbal, and may escalate to physical, kind of like when people at a bar get into a heated argument then start a fist fight.

When you really think about it, without proper knowledge or conditioning, anything that we lack knowledge about can generate fear and trigger the fight or flight response. Consider this, imagine not knowing what a cell phone was, or a TV, and then you heard the cell phone ring or the TV turn on out of the blue. Many of us are conditioned properly with the knowledge that the noises are harmless, so we're not phased by it, but without that knowledge and conditioning, we would immediately go into survival mode and flee; especially if someone was playing Call Of Duty in the other room and you heard gunshots. Without knowing it's a harmless videogame, you would immediately assume the worst. We see similar scenarios in the wild with animals. When we see a bush move abruptly, it does not even phase us because we know it is either the wind or a harmless animal that is more afraid of us than we are of it, but most wild animals are not aware of what is actually in that bush, so they run away without even taking any chances.

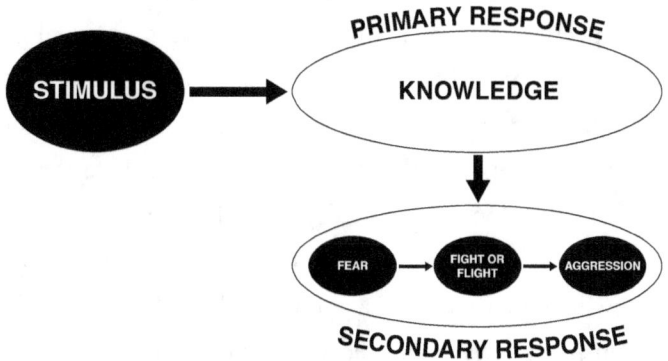

At this point, you're probably asking, "How do I overcome my fears?" Let's refer to this second diagram above; notice how with knowledge, it can override our unconditioned survival responses when exposed to certain stimuli. However, if we start off using our knowledge, and we don't know how to respond properly, our second option could be our basic survival instincts. Think about when you go into a rough neighborhood; you're likely not to walk around alone at night or down any dark alleys. Even if you do your research on the area's crime rates and stuff, deep down, you will not want to take any chances. You may consciously use your knowledge, which is your conditioned primary response, but if someone comes up to you and starts trouble, and you don't have enough knowledge to handle the situation properly, your brain will automatically jump to what is now the secondary response, or your survival instincts.

The important thing to understand from this is that when you have enough knowledge about a certain subject or situation, and you know that it is not a threat to your survival, the stimuli will not trigger your fear in the first place. Think back to when you were just a kid, full of innocence and still figuring the world out. Remember being terrified at night thinking there was a monster under your bed? The fear that if you moved a muscle or stepped down onto the floor, a big, furry hand with menacing claws would reach out, grab your ankle, drag you under, and eat you? I certainly remember those days. What happened, as you got older? You gained an outside perspective and learned that monsters were imaginary, and that the creature under your bed was nothing but an old sweater. When you gained that new knowledge, it reconditioned your thought process and allowed you to understand that there was no immediate threat to your survival, and it was only your perception. This technique can help you overcome not only imaginary fears, but real fears as well. Growing up I had very few imaginary fears as a young child that I conquered before the age of 10, in fact I always enjoyed watching horror movies without any issues while others would cover their eyes and have nightmares; those movies did not scare me because I knew they were not real and I learned to prepare for those kinds of situations.

Real fears, on the other hand, were more common and not as easy to conquer. I did notice, however, that the more knowledge I gained about certain things, the less I feared them. I'm sure many people in the world are afraid of sharks because they hear about rare shark attacks on the news. As a kid, I had a slight fear of sharks, until I watched Shark Week on the Discovery Channel and learned about them. I realized that shark attacks are very uncommon and hard to provoke, and you just need to be in the wrong place at the wrong time. The animals I was always afraid of the most were humans, and the reason for that is because I always felt inferior and I was constantly attacked by people everywhere I went growing up. My low self-esteem made me such an easy target that everybody picked on me. I was always afraid of those people deep down until I learned how people work and that they were just as vulnerable as I was. Like I said earlier, the most common fear is the fear of the unknown, and we can only overcome that by gaining knowledge.

THE RELATIONSHIP BETWEEN INTELLIGENCE AND AGGRESSION

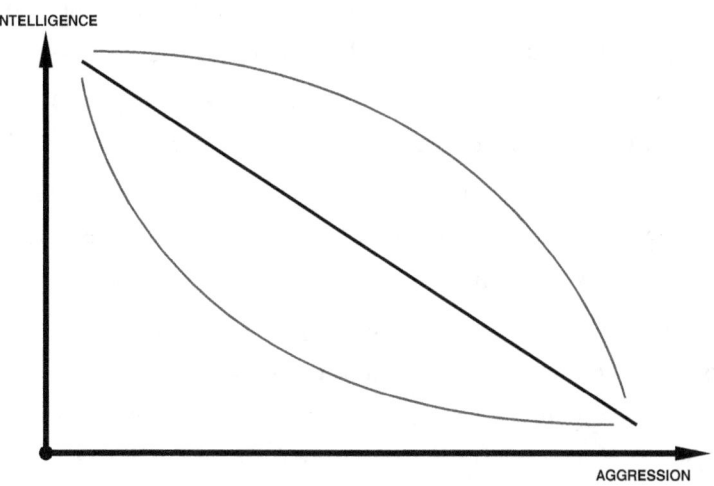

As you can see in the graph above, the relationship between intelligence and aggression is a linear model with a negative slope; this model is not exact or backed up with data, but it is an accurate estimate. As I explained earlier, intelligence can override aggression, so the more knowledge one has about whether or not certain stimuli are a direct threat to his or her survival, the less likely one will be to display aggressive behavior as a primary response. Although the majority of people adhere to the linear model, there are outliers; believe it or not, this world is not perfect.

There are cases where people can be highly intelligent, but they never dealt with certain personal issues or character defects, which gave them a more negative view of the world. These people often display aggressive behavior verbally or passively, often times manipulating others to get what they want. For instance, some people are master manipulators who are nice to people in the beginning to gain their trust only to mess with their emotions and control them later on. Also, there are people who use their intelligence to climb the corporate ladder only to get into a position of power and be able to boss people around. No matter how intelligent a person is, without the right knowledge, like the knowledge from this book, they would still have no way of knowing how the world really is.

On the flip side, there are people who are less intelligent who display kindness and empathy. These people often have self-esteem issues, or they have a more positive view of the world without knowing or understanding the negatives. In many of these cases, these people know what it's like to be hurt, and would never want to do that to others. They often get taken advantage of by others and do not always see it. People like this only display aggressive behavior in more intense situations, otherwise showing stress responses and begging for forgiveness. The truth is, whether a person is an outlier or not, how they act and whether or not they are more intelligent or aggressive depends entirely on their unique experiences. We all have different versions of perceived reality, and they do not always add up to actual reality.

Chapter 7

Perceived Reality vs. Actual Reality

As intelligent as we may be, we are only human, and we are limited to our own knowledge. Our brains are like super computers; they are able to analyze and process everything we encounter in life, and much like computers, we need the information given to us first before we can encode and process. Due to warped perception and the layers of knowledge theory, our personal experiences can have a major influence on our own world, as we know it. The closer you are to that 70:30 ratio, the better outlook you will have on life and the greater your chances of survival will be in today's world. Again, as large and vast as the world is, we as individuals are limited to our own knowledge and experiences. Kind of like a computer or a search engine is limited to the data stored inside of it. After all, it's impossible to know everything because everything is such a broad spectrum. Anyways, there are two basic types of reality; there's perceived reality and actual reality.

PERCEIVED REALITY

Perceived reality is the reality that we believe is real. This form of reality is not "the truth," it is only "our truth"; remember that the truth is only the truth to the best of one's knowledge. Perceived reality is unique yet similar for everyone because even though we're all similar, our experiences differ. It is constantly shaped by our personal life experiences and our responses to our immediate environmental stimuli, and it's based more on what we think and know versus what we really don't know. Perceived reality can blind us from the truth, which can have both positive and negative consequences. For instance, if someone believes that they are doing the right things and that they will be truly successful in life without having to try or work hard, them believing they will be successful will make them feel good, as if they had already achieved their goals. Those great feelings may even boost their self-esteem and make them feel like they have true purpose in life. On the other hand, if they're not doing their research, talking to the right people, or working hard to achieve their goals, chances are they will not be truly successful, and if they are going around screwing other people over to get ahead, they are less likely to be helped or accepted by others which can close doors, making them end up alone and unsuccessful. This is why even though perceived reality can feel comfortable, it's important to take actual reality into consideration if you wish to get anywhere in life.

ACTUAL REALITY

Actual reality is the absolute truth, as we know it, to the best of our knowledge that is. This type of reality is based on all of the years of scientific research and data, documented history, evidence in fossils, logic and reasoning, expert knowledge, and everything discovered and created by human beings over the past many millennia. Things can still change as new scientific discoveries and breakthroughs occur in the future, but the truth, as we know it today, is considered our actual reality. This actual reality is based solely on outer knowledge, and through gaining more outer knowledge, we can get a better grip on reality and start overriding the middle knowledge layer. Understanding more about actual reality is something that helped me heal and grow as a person, and I'm constantly improving myself everyday.

THE BRIDGE / IDEAL REALITY

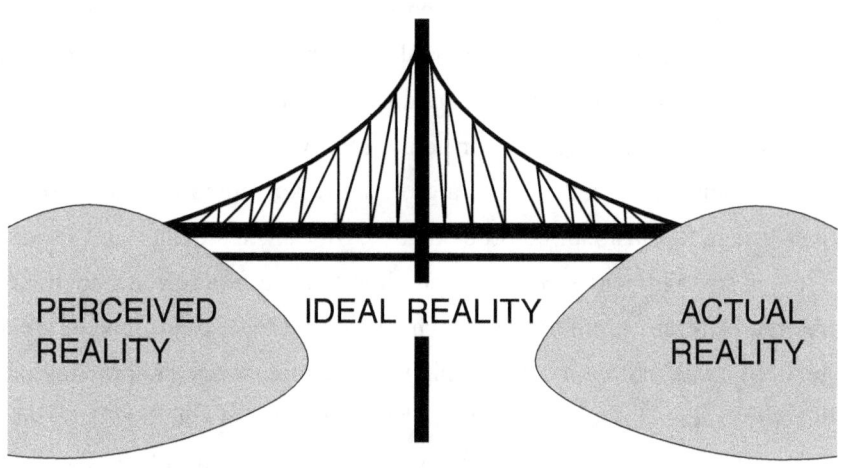

Unfortunately, when it comes to being mentally ill, or in a bad place, many of us are afraid to truly face actual reality; we may say things like, "reality sucks," or simply just feel that way. When we suffer that badly, we tend to warp our realities into something more soothing that helps us get through each and every day. We might even imagine that we are more successful than we are, more powerful than we are, or just in a better place than we are to make ourselves feel good. Then, sadly, somebody always comes along to put us down and remind us of the scary truth, that we're not as successful, powerful, or in as good a place as we thought we were. The feelings are crushing, overwhelming, and hurtful, and it reminds us how pathetic and worthless we feel, even though we're not. Hope tends to be lost, until we go back into our perceived reality and feel better about ourselves again, temporarily. That perceived reality we go back to all the time tends to get lonely after awhile, and it's not as fulfilling as we want it to be. Luckily, there's an even better solution; instead of getting caught up in your perceived reality, make your actual reality better.

Chapter 7

The solution starts off with figuring out what you truly want in life, and trying to imagine how it would feel to be there. In other words, paint a picture of your ideal reality. Just remember that in order for this to really work, your ideal reality must be as realistic as possible, so no superpowers. Sorry... Anyways, let your ideal reality be the bridge you build between your perceived reality and your actual reality. If the idea of your ideal reality excites you, you're off to a great start! Keep in mind that crossing that bridge too fast can be problematic. After all, it's being built as you cross it, so it will take some time and effort to get to where you want to be. As you learn more and figure out what you need to do to bring your ideal reality into actual reality, or mapping out the milestones and drawing the blueprints, the closer you will get to bringing it out of your head and into the world. I will explain more about this later on, but until then, feel free to get excited!

Chapter 8

Things We Can And Cannot Control

Before we create our ideal reality, we must first accept that there are things in life we cannot control. Most of these things we encounter in life may upset us, or even drive us insane, literally! As humans, we have a strong desire for control because the more control we have in life, the more we can benefit ourselves and optimize our chances of survival. However, some people get caught up worrying about what they cannot control, and they waste time stressing over it and trying to change the situation. They will often be very hard on themselves when they do not see their desired outcomes often due to either low self-esteem or egocentrism, having a warped perception, or an alternate sense of reality.

Scenarios can vary, but narcissistic or arrogant people with big egos believe that the world revolves around them, they have a very high sense of entitlement, they care more about themselves than others, and they often have meltdowns when things don't go exactly how they want it. Many might even think, "How dare things not go my way!" or something along the lines of that. On the other hand, people with low self-esteem, like myself for many years, we often care about others more than ourselves, we don't think highly of ourselves, we feel inadequate, and we feel the need to please everyone. When people aren't pleased or get upset with us, we blame ourselves and take things personally, often feeling so overwhelmed and upset, so angry with ourselves as if the world were coming to an end and everyone blamed us. I struggled with those feelings for years, until I did some overall analysis on the many things in life that we can and cannot control.

In order to really be at peace with many situations in life that once baffled us, we must have an understanding of what we truly cannot control and accept it. Some of the major things early in life that we cannot control are the families we are born into, the ways we are raised as children, our upbringings, our immediate environments, what we're taught growing up, the ways we behave as children, who we're surrounded by, how we're treated, etc. Many of us will look at a person who displays negative behavior, or hurts other people, and will just assume that he or she is a bad person. Remember what we learned earlier, that nobody is bad, and there are many external factors that affect a person's personality and make them who they are. Let's face it, if people had a choice to be good from the start, everybody would choose that path, or at least have the intention to. Therefore, a person can never be blamed 100% for their behavior because all they have for elementary foundation is basic animal instincts, and what they learned from their families growing up.

    There are many other things in life that we will never be able to control like weather, traffic, waiting in lines at stores and restaurants, our surrounding environments, the economy, etc. One of the main things that we all wish we could control, but we can't, are the actions of other people. Many of us find it very frustrating when we want certain people we care about to act a certain way or do certain things, but the truth is that they are consciously making those decisions whether others like it or not. As humans, and animals, we all have free will and the ability to make our own choices in life, and we are often influenced by the people we surround ourselves with the most, but we still control our actions.

    Although everything is influenced by our universal inner knowledge, our unique middle and outer knowledge layers play a big role in how we react in certain situations. People will react differently based on the norms they have been accustomed to growing up such as their beliefs, logics, reasoning, and perceptions on life. Many people do not fully understand this concept, and they wonder why people react certain ways in different situations. People with low self-esteem will often blame themselves when others behave certain ways or get upset over things that aren't a big deal.

Things We Can and Cannot Control

Although there are many aspects of life we cannot control, we need to shift our focus away from them and put it towards what we can control. Examples of what we can control in life are things like our actions, our adult lives, our adult decisions, who we become friends with, whether or not we want to stay in a bad situation, whether or not we want help, our reactions to situations, how we handle things, and our lives in general. People will either feel as if they have an internal locus of control or an external locus of control; internal meaning controlled by them and external meaning controlled by others. The truth is that we have absolute control of our lives, but we don't all know how to harness it, and our perceptions can affect the outcomes of our realities. According to the law of attraction, our thoughts emit frequencies that extend out into the universe and attract like frequencies. In other words, our thoughts can manifest and our focuses will become reality.

One concept I always misunderstood was the difference between controlling my own life and controlling other people. First, know that you cannot control the actions of another person, even if you are able to influence them, you will never be able to control them. There is a difference, believe it or not. However, you harness the power to attract what you wish to attract into your life, though it may not always be exact. For example, you may be attracted to a specific person who you wish to build a relationship with and live happily ever after. The issue is, that specific person may not be compatible with you for different reasons that are out of your control, and no matter how bad you want that person to be a certain way that is ideal for you, they will never be willing to conform to your ideal image of them. As much as it sucks, you can never have a successful relationship with that specific person because the fantasy is not real. However, that does not mean you cannot shift your focus to attract a successful relationship with any person into your life, who would be compatible with you. The lesson here is do not waste your energy focusing on desires which are too specific, especially involving social bonds with specific people. Though you cannot control how people are, you can control the types of people you attract into your life by simply changing your mindset.

WE ARE CONTROLLED BY OTHERS UNTIL WE ARE ADULTS

Another concept that is important to grasp is the fact that we have almost no control over our lives until we are 18 years old and out of high school. The day we are born, we are dealt a specific set of cards, and whatever is in our hand we are stuck with no matter what. Though we have no say in the cards we are dealt, we can control how we utilize those cards to find the winning strategy. Think about it this way, you are born into the family you are born into regardless, whether you like it or not. As a kid, you are always told what to do; your parents have rules for you, your families influence you with their beliefs and perceptions of the world, you are forced to go to school and do homework, authority figures at school give you detention if you misbehave, and you are peer pressured by other kids your age or older. You are told when to go to bed, what to eat, what to wear, how to act, what religion to practice, and on top of all that, you are trying to figure out the world while learning to adapt to your immediate environment to optimize your chance of survival.

Basically, others control your life when you are a child, and you are simply just taking in what is given to you because you assume it is the way to survive. We often do not realize how much people are truly influenced by others around them and the way others treat them. Many people do not have a fair advantage in life while others do. Think about it this way; when you're born into the world, you are a computer with a clean hard drive. The only data, or software, on that hard drive is the basic essentials of what you need to survive; in other words, your inner knowledge. The people you interact with the most (family, friends, relatives, community, etc.) are the users, or the programmers. What people do not always realize is that when children look up to them, they have a lot of influence over those children. In fact, they are programming those children, or computers, to do certain things. Computers will perform tasks given to them by programmers assuming it is what they need to do. People and animals are the same way until they become self-sufficient and intelligent enough to form their own beliefs.

So, if a programmer programs a computer to do bad things, is it the computer's fault? No! Even though the computer executed the task, the programmer influenced the computer to do so. Just like when children have parents, older siblings, etc. who influence them with their actions. Even though the children consciously make the decision to mimic what they see, the parents, older siblings, etc. influenced those actions. The child's brain will assume automatically that mimicking what others do will boost their chances of survival, so be careful what you teach to your kids or expose them to.

THE CROSS ROADS OF LIFE

Even though we have no control over our lives as children, we gain full control of our lives once we turn 18 and finish high school. As a kid, growing up always scared me because I had all of these adults in my life telling me how much harder life gets as you grow up and how it just gets worse. It was not until I became an adult myself that I learned the real truth. Life can either get better or worse as you grow up, it just depends on the path you take. I wish someone told me that when I was a kid. As a child, life can be a rather bumpy road as you struggle to learn the ways of the world and get through the tough years, but once you hit age 18 and graduate high school, you come to a major milestone known as the cross roads of life. When you reach the cross roads of life, it divides into two paths, and you can go either way; you can either go up to road of success, or down to the road of failure. No matter how life was growing up, you always have absolute control over which path you choose.

The road of success is a long journey that involves many bumps, potholes, and hurdles. At first, it may seem like you have chosen the wrong path, until you realize that you start feeling a little bit better after overcoming each obstacle; that is called progress. With this road, the struggles are only temporary, and they shape you into the person you will be in the future. In other words, they build character and give you what you need to survive. There comes a time where you reach a mountain, and once you do, you climb that mountain, which takes time, hard work, and dedication. Eventually, you reach the top of that mountain, and that is where you peak in life, and become the best person you can be. You optimize happiness and success and look back on your struggles with a sense of pride. If you make good choices in life, gain outside perspectives, treat others with respect, confront and deal with all of your problems, develop a positive mindset, build healthy relationships, pursue your ideal career path, achieve financial security and stability, and engage in healthy and enjoyable activities, you will achieve true happiness and success, and life will be easier.

The road of failure is a long journey as well, only these struggles will not be temporary. In fact, this road is covered with obstacles that only lead to more and more obstacles that just get worse. Things can spiral out of control as you keep going further down into the dark depths of this path, and eventually, you end up in deep trenches that have nothing but quicksand on the bottoms of them. You definitely do not want to get to that quicksand, because if you do, it is very difficult to come out of it. If you do not confront your underlying issues, deal with your character defects, or have positive relationships with people, and you end up having a negative mindset, resorting to self-harm, turning to substance abuse, settling in a

Things We Can and Cannot Control

dead end job that you hate, and/or get involved in a life of crime, you will fail. You will see the darkest sides of reality, and life will be very difficult for you.

I know the road of failure sounds terrifying because it is, and that's a fact. You do not have to choose that path. You're childhood is chosen for you by the families you are born into, do not let anyone choose your adulthood for you. No matter what, you need to do what is best for you, and find your way. It is all of our duties to make a positive contribution to society, and what we get in return will be very fulfilling if we work it properly.

The first part of our journey together has now come to an end. Now that you have a basic understanding of how people work and why society is the way that it is, we can move on and embark on the second part of our journey where we will learn what we can do to improve ourselves, help others, improve society, and ultimately, lead us all down the road of salvation. After all, that mountain is huge, and it has plenty of room! Let's move on to the next phase!

PART II

WHAT WE CAN DO TO MAKE A POSITIVE CHANGE

Chapter 9

The Next Phase In Our Journey

Hey, there! I am happy that you have made it this far! Welcome to the second phase in our journey, as we are delighted to have you. We still have a bit of a way to go, but the beginning is the most difficult part. Once you get passed that, it will almost be smooth sailing. Of course, you need to keep in mind that life is not perfect, and that issues are bound to occur along this journey. However, the key is to know how to respond to those issues and resolve them properly. Remember, "A" is for "Adapt," not "Avoid." Avoiding certain issues can allow them to accumulate, and even magnify over time, which ultimately leads to newer and greater issues.

In this phase of our journey, I will teach you the methods and techniques I have developed myself in order to help pave the road to a happier life. It's still a work in progress, but I have a clear vision, or blue print, of the life I want. I've designed the bridge of my ideal reality, and it involves helping others just like you do the same. You will learn some of the best ways to help yourself, help others, and help society as a whole, but it must be done in that order because you can not fully help others until you have fully helped yourself first. That was a hard lesson for me to learn. I always put others before myself for most of my life, and almost every time, I was screwed over, taken advantage of, left with nothing in return, and, of course, in a serious rut that I thought I'd never get out of. It was not until I had to be hospitalized twice for attempting suicide, and after a year of trying different things, and drinking a lot, that I finally decided I needed to take care of myself.

There is a way to create a healthier society, but it will take all of our participation for it to really work, or at least a good majority of us. We must learn to take an honest look at ourselves, and find our flaws and character defects. Then, we must do what it takes to fix them, and find the happiness we all want and deserve. We also need to look at the way we treat others, no matter who they are, what they look like, what they've done, or where they are at in life. Many of us do not see that we contribute to a lot of society's problems whether we realize it or not. We forget that something as simple as a smile or a "thank you" can make a huge difference in someone else's day or life. Remember what we learned in the first phase of our journey, it's not as simple as people being either just good or bad. Everyone has their reasons for being the way they are. When we hurt others for acting a certain way, we perceive what we are doing as right and just, but on their end, they are being beat down more after already being beaten down in life. We don't need to reward negative behavior, but we also don't need to keep re-opening another person's wounds. Never give someone more than they deserve, good or bad. It's time that society accepts some responsibility for labeling certain people and preventing them from healing. In order for society to improve, a positive chain reaction must be started.

 I did not point that out to make anyone feel guilty, my goal is to make everyone more aware of the potential damage they may be causing. Once you become aware, you will learn and know better, then you will make better decisions in the future. I am definitely guilty of hurting people who have hurt me first. I immediately jumped to the conclusion that they were the scum of the earth and that they deserved to suffer and die, but I realized later on that they were already suffering in the first place and I was making their suffering worse. Remember how our parents always told us "two wrongs don't make a right" when we were kids? Well, there is a lot of truth to that. Let's take my abusive ex-girlfriend, for example, she did a real number on me and traumatized me for years. She actually did apologize to me months after we broke up, but I completely told her off and said really mean things to her. I was proud of myself at the time because I thought I was doing the right thing. However, in the bigger picture, I was abusing someone who had already been badly abused in life, and if someone saw what I said to her from an outside perspective, they would

The Next Phase In Our Journey

think I was the bad guy. That is why it is important to take every side of a story into consideration before passing any judgment. After all, you never know what the other person experienced or how it affected them.

I have now chosen to think of others and watch what I say or do. No matter how nasty someone might be to me, I don't take it personally, and I wish him or her the best in life. As we get deeper into this phase of our journey, you will learn the best methods for dealing with toxic people, which is a major part of your own recovery. Speaking of your recovery, let's take care of you first, and worry about others later. Who knows, they could be reading my book right now too! Let's keep on moving!

Chapter 10

Time To Get Motivated!

The first step to living a happier life is to understand and accept that you have issues, and get motivated to move passed them. They say that this can be one of the hardest things to do sometimes, but it is necessary in order to make positive changes and feel better. Remember what we learned earlier about the human body, it has evolved to be able to constantly adapt, heal, regenerate, and balance, and it is the external factors in our environment that make the largest contribution to our states of well being. However, there are also internal factors, which are fueled by the external. I will explain further later on. Right now, I need to get you motivated to want a better life for yourself.

Many might ask questions like, "How do I get motivated?" "Where do I start?" "Is it possible for me to be happy?" "Do I even deserve to be happy?" If you have asked any of these questions, or similar questions, you are in the right place! I struggled to find motivation for many years, both intrinsic and extrinsic. I had to rebuild my life from scratch many times as well. Many people kept telling me, "Stop being so depressed!" "You're choosing to be miserable!" "Just get over it, your life's not that hard!" "Just choose to be happy, why is that so hard?" Many people don't realize how certain illnesses like depression or PTSD work, and how they can get our minds into unhealthy patterns that we don't know how to break out of. I was unable to break those unhealthy patterns until I realized that motivation is a lot like Newton's law of inertia.

Newton's law of inertia states that an object at rest will stay at rest, and an object in motion will stay in motion; unless acted on by an opposing force. What do you need to do? You need to find your opposing force. Your opposing force can be any people, places, or things that will either be the friction to get you out of motion in an unhealthy pattern or direction, or the push or pull you need to get you out of a state of rest and into the right direction, or both. There are many of these effective "opposing forces" out there that could do that for you, you just need to be willing to find them or let them come to you. It could be something as simple as a person convincing you or forcing you to get help, a good song to get the blood flowing, or maybe even just hitting rock bottom and not wanting to be there ever again. The best you can do is work with what, or who, you've got already.

Keep in mind that you are not getting better for anyone else other than yourself. If you need to let someone else be your motivation, it could benefit you in the short-term to get you started. Just be very careful with that, because when I did that after hitting rock bottom, the people I wanted to get better for turned their backs on me and betrayed me. The key here is to make sure you have people who will help you and have your back, because you need that support. If you have nobody, there are places you can turn to in order to meet the right people. I will discuss that later on as well. The extrinsic sources of motivation will be able to build your intrinsic sources as you grow and build yourself up. It's like being an injured animal that needs to be nurtured back to health in order to be self-sufficient again and survive. Remember, you have the right to be weak, and admitting it will make you strong.

Once you become aware of your issues, get motivated, and make the decision to improve your life, you have just conquered the most difficult part of the journey. Now, it is time to work on not only developing a more positive mindset, but also taking action towards those goals. You will be amazed what you learn along the way, and these amazing discoveries could be your next Aha moments. It is important to give yourself the time you need to heal, for there is no major rush. Don't worry, that time will fly by before you know it! Just keep doing the next right thing, and allow good people with experience to guide you.

Chapter 11

Reach Out For Help!

One of the most difficult things for people to do is reach out for help. Let's face it, nobody wants to admit that they are vulnerable, but when they spend years holding that back, they become very self-destructive and destroy a lot of good relationships. Although it is scary at first to open up, I promise you that you will feel so much better afterwards.

There are many reasons why people don't get help such as they may lack the guidance and support they truly need, they might have an ego that they refuse to surrender, they are unaware of the help that is out there, they could have moderate or severe trust issues, they could have the fear of paradigm shifts or stepping out of comfort zones, they may feel truly alone in the world and that nobody will understand or people will judge, or maybe they were manipulated their whole lives with the belief that help is for the weak or simply just a punishment. There are many other examples, but whatever the reasons may be, it is important to overcome them and get help as soon as possible.

In order for the healing to begin, you must surrender with complete honesty, but make sure to surrender to the right people. If you talk to the wrong people, they could make you feel even worse about yourself, especially if you lack the real knowledge you need. You must convince yourself that it is okay to reach out for help, and that admitting you are weak will make you strong and brave. After all, like I mentioned earlier, we all depend on each other for survival from an evolutionary standpoint. If you want a better life for yourself, short term and long term, you must be willing to do whatever it takes to get better and overcome your problems. I know it sounds intimidating, but I am here to walk you through it. I am going to show you some of the many key resources available to you to start your own personal journey to happiness and success.

Chapter 11

FRIENDS AND FAMILY

Friends and family are not always the best people to start with, but that depends entirely on your unique situation. Some people are blessed with amazing friends and loving families, while others only have fake friends and broken families. Whatever your situation may be, it is good to work with what you've already got, but there is a proper method to dealing with friends and family. First, you must know that not everybody will fully understand what you are going through, and some people might judge. Also, not everybody can comprehend or handle the burden of having you vent all of your problems to them. I was guilty of making that very mistake of only going to friends and family for that kind of help and support. Later, I realized that I had pushed them all away. They could not help me, and it was not because they were mean, it was because they did not know how to deal with my issues, let alone their own issues they may have had.

Friends and family do not always have the knowledge and wisdom that the professionals do, so they are not the best people to go to for your major issues. When people don't know what to say or how to help you, they may mislead you even though they are doing their best to help. Some people might even make you feel worse about yourself, so you really need to be careful whom you tell certain things. Also, keep in mind that if you tell personal secrets to friends and family, they are not obligated to keep those secrets, and they could slip up and tell someone one of these days. I know you would not want that to happen. So, whether you already have a good support network, or you have absolutely nobody to turn to, I will share with you the best places to start.

START WITH THERAPY OR COUNSELING

The best place to start getting help is by seeing a therapist or counselor and having one-on-one sessions. The one-on-one sessions are critical if you are not yet used to opening up in front of people because it may be unsettling at first. There are many places where you can seek therapy or counseling. If you are currently in school, whether it be elementary school, middle school, high school, or even college, you have guidance counselors available to you who you can make appointments with. You could also seek therapy outside of school at the many offices all over the place where you can reach out and set something up.

The key with a therapist is not only to make sure they take your health insurance, but also to connect with them on a personal but professional level. Remember, it is strictly a doctor/patient relationship. Much like any relationship, you need to build trust and feel comfortable with the person you will be sharing your life story with. This was something that was frightening for me because of my major trust issues, but I kept in mind that what you tell a therapist is under doctor/patient confidentiality, so they are legally obligated to keep your secrets. My recommendation for beginners is to start off by getting to know your therapist and only tell him or her things you would normally tell anybody. This is a way that you can get comfortable with your therapist and build that trust. Depending on your personal needs and preferences, you may not always click with the right therapist at first, but once you find one you click with, you can start small and get deeper as you build the relationship. Keep in mind that therapists have heard it all, so nothing you say will offend them or scare them. Just make sure that their credentials fit your personal needs.

If you are a minor, and you need parents' permission to seek therapy or counseling, it is totally understandable if your parents won't let you because that is out of your control. Unfortunately, they have a right to believe whatever they want and influence you with those same beliefs.

However, once you are over the age of 18, you are a legal adult with the power to make your own decisions. If you are still a minor, and your parents won't let you get help from a therapist, your best bet will be to seek help from your school counselor, or any trustworthy adult at school who can help you. After all, most people hate seeing children get abused, and many professionals who work at schools are mandated reporters for child abuse. Trust me, they will be happy to help you any way they can.

OUTPATIENT TREATMENT CENTERS

Although one-on-one therapy is incredibly beneficial, it may not be enough for some people. Another thing you could look into are outpatient partial hospital programs or treatment centers. These programs typically consist of group therapy with a team of counselors counseling everyone in the same room while encouraging people to interact with and support one another. You may also be able to engage in different activities to either keep your mind occupied or help you identify and work through your issues. You will need support from others to heal effectively, so what better way of getting support than from those who have been in similar places as you who will understand what your are going through. Doing work in groups was a major turning point for me, it taught me that I really was not alone, and that so many people struggle with issues similar to mine, and even worse than mine.

Another benefit to doing therapy in a group is the fact that you can make new friends. Of course, you need to be careful who you make friends with because you never know the kinds of people they are, or if they could get you involved in a bad situation. At this point in your journey, where you are in a rough place, you may benefit from connecting with people you meet in these programs, especially if you have nobody in your life. The key is to be smart and get to know them first. It is nice to know that you are really not alone, but I will get more in depth later on about the dynamics and structures of friendships and relationships that make them work. Aside from that, much like one-on-one therapy, you need to make sure that the structures and credentials of these programs fit your personal recovery needs.

INPATIENT TREATMENT CENTERS

Inpatient treatment centers are always there when you need them. These consist of psychiatric units, mental hospitals, rehabilitation centers, detox centers, halfway houses, etc. If you need inpatient treatment for a time to recover from addiction, alcoholism, suicide attempts, depression, etc., by all means, do it. These places not only allow you to meet other people in similar situations, but you are under 24-hour watch by the staff who is there to take care of you and keep you safe.

The first time I had to be put in a psychiatric unit, I was a little nervous because I did not know what to expect. I had tried to commit suicide the night before, and I was taken to the hospital the next day. The doctors and nurses at the hospital took great care of me, and it felt so good to be honest with them and tell them what happened the night before. It was like I did not have to hide it anymore. I needed a psychological evaluation to determine whether or not I needed to spend time in a psych unit, and it turned out that I did. When I arrived at the psych unit, I was escorted to my room and welcomed with open arms and smiles by the very friendly staff and other patients. They had all different kinds of activities to participate in, and I chose to participate in all of them because I believe the best way to heal is to have an open mind.

If you ever do need to spend time in a psychiatric unit or a rehabilitation facility, take as much time as you need to fully recover. Be sure to set all other priorities aside, and make health your number one focus. The less stress you have weighing on your mind, the faster you will recover, and the less likely you will relapse. Remember, help is all around you, and all you need to do is be honest and ask for it. Be willing to try new things you have not tried before, as long as they are healthy and positive. No matter how frivolous they may seem, you never know what will actually work for you.

FELLOWSHIPS AND TWELVE STEP PROGRAMS

Joining any kind of fellowship is not only a great way to meet others like you and make new friends, but it is also a great way to start if you do not have the financial means to see a therapist first. Although seeing a therapist one-on-one first is ideal, I understand that not everyone can afford it. These fellowships, such as alcoholics anonymous, narcotics anonymous, overeaters anonymous, codependents anonymous, love addicts anonymous, sex addicts anonymous, etc., are all self supporting through their own contributions with no dues or fees. It is different because you speak in front of a whole group of people, which can be intimidating at first, but luckily, anonymity is a core tradition of all those fellowships, so nobody gossips or criticizes. Also, they have all had similar struggles as you, so they know what it's like.

A great thing to keep in mind is that you are in no way obligated to speak at your first meeting. If you are a beginner, the best way to start out would be to listen to other peoples' shares until you feel comfortable. Then, when you are ready, start off by sharing things you would normally share with anybody, just like you would with a new therapist. Once you get comfortable in a certain group of people, you may open up more if you wish.

When it comes to working the twelve steps, your best bet would be to get a sponsor. A sponsor is somebody within the fellowship with wisdom, experience, and at least a year of sobriety. You can build a good relationship with your sponsor if you connect well, and they will be happy to support you, talk to you, and walk you through the steps. The twelve steps are an incredibly effective way to uncover the roots of your spiritual emptiness; they basically allow you to admit that your addiction is too much for you to handle, surrender to a higher power, learn more about yourself and why you are the way you are, have the opportunity to become a better person and make amends with people you've harmed, and ultimately, practice the principles you have learned and help other addicts who still suffer.

I will tell you that joining the AA fellowship was one of the best decisions I made in my entire life. I was able to free myself from the power alcohol had over me, and now I have more time in my life for greater things such as family and success. Most people wait until they are in their 30s, 40s, 50s, 60s, etc. to start handling those kinds of issues. However, I made the choice to start handling them in my early 20s, and I encourage others like me to do the same. When you first join a fellowship, you must be willing to be proactive and surrender knowing that you will be much happier once you get through this paradigm shift. When you get a sponsor, he or she will help you with everything, and you will make lots of great connections along the way. Again, just be careful whom you connect with, like I said about the outpatient treatment centers.

OTHER NATURAL METHODS OF HEALING

There are many other natural forms of healing out there that you could try such as yoga, meditation, exercise, Reiki, acupuncture, massages, other therapies, etc. If you have an open mind, you can open up a whole new world of healing for yourself and be willing to try some of these methods. What is most important about using any of these methods is that you truly believe it will work for you because if you do, it will actually work. Your mind is incredibly powerful, and you would be amazed what it can do.

Of course there are certain external factors that affect you physically as well such as diet, exercise, breathing, and sleep, but there is one major aspect of internal factors that could prevent your healing as well, like I mentioned previously. It might sound rather complex, but it's really not. The main internal factors that affect your healing are vertebral subluxations. This simply refers to misalignments in your spinal vertebrae. It might sound crazy, but think about this, your nervous system consists of your brain, your spinal cord, and all of your nerves, which control everything in your body. All of the main nerves in your body branch off from your spinal cord and then branch off even further all over. Your spinal cord is then protected and supported by the 24 vertebrae that create your spine. What many people don't realize is that we encounter daily stressors that cause these subluxations, or misalignments, and they can worsen over time if not corrected. When the vertebrae are misaligned, they pinch those main nerves branching out of your spinal cord and to other places in your body, causing interrupted nerve flow.

According to chiropractors, since vertebral subluxations interrupt nerve flow, they can be the leading cause of most ailments in your body. In fact, I learned all of this incredible wisdom from my chiropractor. I was skeptic about it at first, but after he explained it to me, it made sense, and I decided to give it a try to see how it would work for me. Next thing you know, in just a few months, many little ailments I had most of my life went away. It was truly remarkable, and it became part of my natural lifestyle. Unfortunately, I know that not everyone can afford to go to a chiropractor, but luckily, there are different exercises you could do to maintain a healthy spine, along with inversion therapy where you just hang upside down for a few minutes.

Although maintaining a healthy spine and minimizing vertebral subluxations is the key to optimize your physical health, it is not enough to optimize your mental health alone. There are still external factors that you need to balance you out mentally aside from food, water, and oxygen.

I will explain more later on about what it really takes to optimize mental health, but definitely keep a healthy spine, eat right, exercise, and try some of those different healing methods!

MEDICATION

If you are struggling badly, there are options for different medications out there that can help stabilize your brain chemistry. However, medications can have lots of harmful side effects, so only consider them as a last resort. If you need medication, especially if your only other option was to go insane or harm yourself, by all means do it. Just make sure you know that medication should only be a short-term solution, not a long-term solution. The real goal is to have you be able to live the life you deserve without the use of chemical substances, but medication can be a stepping-stone to get you in a better place.

When it comes to taking your medication, make sure you follow your psychiatrist's orders and work with him or her on a regular basis. Get regular blood work to make sure your medication is not harming you in any way. When it comes time to get off your medications, do it slowly and by the doctor's orders because coming off too fast or going cold turkey can be very dangerous. Just like everything else, always be cautious and go with your gut feeling.

OTHER OPTIONS TO HOLD YOU OVER

If you are ever in a situation where nobody is around, and you feel alone and in a bad place, you can always phone a friend or a person you trust. Once you build a good support network, you will have multiple options in case certain people are busy or away from the phone. If all else fails, you can always call the National Suicide Prevention Lifeline at **1-800-273-8255**; they are available 24 hours a day. Don't be afraid to reach out!

Chapter 12

Do An Overall Analysis Of Your Life

This is the part in your journey where you need to take massive action. Now that you know some of the many resources available to you, you need to make sure to utilize them properly. It is very important to understand that in order to do an overall analysis of your life, you will need the help of a person or people with an outside perspective. Remember that you are limited to your own knowledge and life experiences until you gain that outside perspective. When choosing these individuals, make sure to choose wisely because biased opinions should not matter to you, but credible opinions should.

For example, I had people in my own family tell me there was nothing wrong with me when I thought I had PTSD, but once I started seeing a therapist, I was officially diagnosed with it. The key here is that therapists have credible opinions because they are professionals with lots of knowledge and experience, but when your family members try to tell you otherwise, you need to ask yourself, "Is this person a therapist? Does this person have any kind of knowledge or wisdom in the field of psychology?" If not, that person has a biased opinion. No matter who they are, or whether or not they actually have your best interest at heart, keep in mind that all people are limited to their own knowledge and experiences. Plus, they could have warped perceptions. I know it can be tough when it comes to our families or our parents. After all, they are the biggest influences in our lives early on, but make sure to only trust credible opinions no matter what.

Now, let's go back to the overall analysis. In order for this to work, you must be totally honest with the credible people you are working with, and you need to be willing to hear the real truths. As much as the truth hurts, it is not something you can avoid because if you avoid it, it definitely will not benefit you in the long run. Remember how I talked about perceived reality versus actual reality, and "the bridge" of ideal reality? This is one of the ways to start building that bridge to turn your ideal reality into actual reality. Also, remember that you need to be willing to do whatever it takes to get healthy, even if you need to make some tough decisions. With doing this analysis, whether it is with your therapist, your sponsor, both, or any other credible people you trust, you need to uncover the external factors in your life that are keeping you imbalanced. These external factors could be relationships, partnerships, friendships, living situations, jobs, or any other kinds of interactions with people. The key here is to figure out what unhealthy situations you might be in that you need to remove yourself from in order to be able to heal. I will share with you my strategies, or "escape plans" for getting out of certain situations properly.

GETTING OUT OF AN UNHEALTHY LIVING SITUATION

Removing yourself from an unhealthy living situation is the most important thing you can do for your mental health because your place of living is where you spend the majority of your time, along with having all of your stuff there. It is supposed to be a home, so if it does not feel that way, it is time to move on. Like I had mentioned in Chapter 3, sometimes people get stuck in unhealthy living situations because the costs of living are very high and not everyone can afford to live on their own. Whether your situation is having abusive or neglectful parents, domestic violence, an unhealthy relationship, substance abuse, household conflicts, being too crowded, being alone, etc., you need to do what's best for you and make a positive change. Being in an unhealthy living situation harms your mental health because you are simply just adapting to that unhealthy environment. You need to be more on edge or dulled down to survive.

Do An Overall Analysis Of Your Life

Whatever your situation may be, you need to form an escape plan. If you can afford to live on your own, do it as soon as possible because it will be worth the money for you to have a safe place to go at the end of each day. If you need to take in roommates, by all means, do it. Make sure you choose your roommates wisely because you want them to be compatible with you, and make sure you can handle living with them. If you cannot afford to live on your own yet, this is where you will need to get creative. You need to utilize all available resources you have to get you into a safer and healthier living situation. The best place to start would be friends and family, because the good ones will be more than happy to help you in a time of need if they can. Just always be sure to respect their boundaries and house rules. What you need to understand is that if you need to live with someone else to get out of an unhealthy situation, you should look at it as temporary or transitional because it would not be fair to the other person or people for you to mooch off of them forever. Always work towards self-sufficiency, it's the best way to survive.

If the unhealthy situation you are trying to get out of is an abusive situation, whether it's with a parent, sibling, friend, or relationship partner, your best bet would either be to go behind their backs to make those escape plans, or, in more severe cases, call the local authorities and report them. Remember, nobody has the right to abuse you or hurt you, no matter who they are. It can be a very difficult thing to do, but that's how you need to take your power back from them. If you have nowhere to go after that, you could always look into shelters for battered men or women. You would be surrounded by others who have been in similar places, and I'm sure they would be happy to support you.

If you happen to be homeless and have nowhere to go, that can be a tough place to be. After all, many people in those situations try panhandling and depending on the kindness of others to survive. Unfortunately, not many people give to these poor, helpless individuals who struggle, and while some might have no compassion for people beneath their socio-economic status, others are most likely either just shy, afraid, or they don't carry cash on them anymore. That can be quite common in a world of credit cards and electronic currency.

If you find yourself in a situation where you are homeless and panhandling, especially if you develop a problem with substance abuse, you need to contact the hundreds of organizations in your area that help people in your situation. You might get some no's before you get a yes, so keep pushing for it. This is a good time to drop your ego and put your pride aside, and it's okay because we depend on each other to survive. I recently started handing out that kind of contact information to the panhandlers I see when I am out driving. If you have no access to that contact information, I recommend going to a local library and using their computers to do a Google search. If you need to utilize any resources recommended in Chapter 11 for your mental and physical health, such as a rehab, detox, psych unit, hospital, etc., do whatever it takes to get yourself healthy again. Always make health number one, and then you can work with people who will help you get your life back together. Help is all around you, and it is entirely up to you whether or not you want to ask for it.

Whatever your unhealthy living situation may be, just get creative and do what you need to do to get out of it. If you have professionals and other credible people telling you that your living situation is unhealthy, even if you do not see it, trust them because they may see what you don't. That is why an outside perspective is so important. Another major thing you need to realize is that when you first get out of the unhealthy situation, you will need some time to heal or to adapt to a healthier environment. When you are so used to constantly being on edge because you feel in danger, it's because your brain was conditioned that way, and you can only be reconditioned if you change your environment and gain that outside perspective, along with the support you truly need.

GETTING OUT OF A JOB YOU HATE

Aside from your living situation, being in a healthy work environment is just as important because you spend much of your time there too. I think it's safe to say that most people have had at east one job in their lives that they could not stand. I know a lot of people have a hard time holding onto jobs because they are never satisfied. This is an area in which you really need to find yourself and figure out what is best for you. I will talk more about career building later on. Right now, I am talking about short-term solutions to get you into the next chapter in your life. We do not always realize how our jobs affect our self-esteem, or even our mental and physical health. Sometimes we even feel trapped as if we have no choice but to continue working somewhere we are unhappy. However, that is not the case.

The truth is, yes, we all need to make money in order to cover our costs of living and pay our bills, but there is more than just one way to earn that money. Let's face it, if there was only one job in the whole world, our economy would go to turmoil, and nothing else would drive it. Of course, your long-term goal should always be to keep advancing yourself and work towards your career path with something you truly want to do in life, but I will get more in depth with that later on. For a short-term solution, you need to find something that will benefit you in the short-term, and maybe even prepare you for the long-term. Always think long-term no matter what. When choosing a better job for the short-term, make sure it fits both your financial and personal needs.

When it comes to the job you are currently in, the one you hate, you need to form an escape plan, and get out of there smoothly without putting yourself in a bad position. There are many people out there, who stop caring, and they try to get fired, or they quit on the spot. That is something that can come back and bite you later on, especially when you need references. The proper way to do it is to start off by searching for other jobs. You can do so by looking online, asking around, using referrals and contacts, or even submitting new applications. This is a way to secure yourself financially, and set you up for transitioning to the new job. Do you hate being mistreated by your asshole boss? Well the only real power he or she has over you is the fact that he or she is paying you money, so once you can earn money elsewhere, you can take away the power that boss has over you.

Once you are all set with another job, and you have secured yourself financially, you are ready to move on. Make sure you actually do an interview or at least some kind of orientation first to make sure it is a good fit for you, or if you go the entrepreneurship route, make sure that you will be able to stream sustainable revenue and handle the reality of the situation. Once you can guarantee the new job, you can then discard the old one by putting in your two weeks resignation notice. Putting in your two weeks is common courtesy because you give your boss or managers time to compensate with scheduling the employees they will still have, and maybe even hire someone new to replace you. No matter what, any good, credible person will wish you the best of luck with whatever comes next, and only the nasty, miserable people will have feelings of bitterness towards you, but that's their issue, not yours. No matter how bitter or nasty anyone is, always respond with kindness. Simply just shake hands and say, "thank you, it's been a pleasure working with you." Then move on. Showing that kind of respect will always reward you no matter what because let's face it, you never know if you will ever need something to fall back on or if your old boss gets transferred to your new work place. Always end on a good note, and keep a positive mindset moving forward. If you can do that, you will have no issues at all.

YOUR OVERALL RELATIONSHIPS WITH OTHERS

In order to totally transform your life into the life you want and deserve, you really need to take a look at all of the relationships you have with others. Whether they are close friends, significant others, coworkers, friends you see on occasion, or even just acquaintances, those relationships have an effect on you and your health. They say that you become the people you surround yourself with most, and that is due to mob mentality. Like attracts like and birds of a feather flock together, so your survival instincts tell you that if you want to be accepted by certain people, you need to act a certain way. The key is to make sure you will be doing things that benefit you as well. Ideally, in any relationship, both people should benefit somehow. There are many different kinds of relationships among people that I have observed over the course of my life.

In addition, one of the most important things to keep in mind, something I neglected to do for many years, is that no matter what, you always need to take care of yourself first. Now, don't get me wrong, helping people is a wonderful thing to do, it's something I've always enjoyed doing myself, but there are a lot of people out there who may take advantage of your kindness for their own benefit. I've had this happen to me so many times in the past, and it kept setting me back from getting ahead, and I would always end up badly hurt in some way. What I learned from my many experiences is that if someone is hurting me more than I'm helping them, they are depleting my resources faster than I can replenish. This kind of imbalance can put a person in a position where they can't help others or themselves at all because they will have nothing left to give. It's like constantly lighting a candle without replacing the wax or the wick, it gets burnt out.

Take this, for example, how do animals in the wild go extinct? People kill them off and use their resources faster than they can repopulate. What happens when too many cows graze in the same pasture? The grass is eaten faster than it can regrow, so eventually those cows will have no food left, and they could starve. Here's a more human related example: what happens when someone constantly asks you for money faster than you can save or earn it? That's right! You end up with an empty bank account. These scenarios are each an example of a tragedy of the commons, which is when a resource is depleted faster than it can replenish; it runs out simply because the supply cannot keep up with the demand.

Relationships with people who do this are very unhealthy, and they never end well. I learned that there are givers and takers in this world. Givers care more about others and are willing to give and help people any way they can, and they often give back when others help them. Takers, on the other hand, care more about themselves, and they take from others without giving back, often leaving and moving on when a person is sucked dry and has nothing left to give. We must understand that takers are not bad people, they just learned how to survive this way and they don't know anything else, and sadly, they often never find true happiness unless they learn to give. In nature, we see three main types of symbiotic relationships; parasitism, mutualism, and commensalism.

Parasitism is a relationship in which two organisms interact, and one benefits on behalf of harming the other. A great example in nature would be a tick clinging to an animal, sucking blood, and transmitting diseases. In relationships among humans, we often see this behavior involving either two takers or a giver and a taker; a person could use someone for money, sex, a place to live, etc., and they live off that person while causing them harm in some way. With two takers, they're both using each other and harming each other and themselves. This kind of symbiotic relationship is a very unhealthy one.

Mutualism is when two organisms are constantly helping each other out in some way, and they both benefit. In nature, we see this with smaller fish that live in the mouth of a shark; the fish helps the shark by eating the left over food out of its teeth keeping its mouth healthy, and the shark helps the fish by offering it food and protection from predators. In human relationships, we see this kind of behavior between two givers, like when two people are constantly teaming up, helping each other out, and both benefiting. A great modern day example would be driving someone to a place going in the same direction you're going in, and they give you gas money.

Commensalism is like a form of parasitism; only the organism that benefits is not harming the other in any way. There are lots of organisms in nature that may coexist in this type of way, like offspring who depend on their parents for survival, but the parents aren't harmed because they love their offspring. With humans, you may see a multi-millionaire who lends his friend five dollars every week to buy a cup of coffee, but giving up five dollars every week will not even put a dent in a millionaire's bank account. Although this kind of symbiotic relationship does no harm, it is not exactly fair.

If you're helping someone, and they are not helping you or taking your feelings into consideration, you must tell yourself, "I'm a person too, and my feelings matter." Understand that a person like that is not worth helping, especially if they're causing you harm in any way. You are not responsible for their happiness, and you most likely will be unable to fix them. All you can do is part ways and wish them the best. If you feel like you've failed that person, don't worry because you didn't. Their problems have nothing to do with you and their actions are out of your control. Chances are, they will turn out fine and get the help they need from the right sources, or they might stay in their predicaments until they realize they're going down the wrong path. Leave it to me to show those misguided folks the way to true happiness in life, and put your focus on you to allow yourself the time and support you need to heal. After all, you are just as important as they are.

Chapter 12

PARTING WAYS WITH TOXIC PEOPLE

Finally, when you complete the overall analysis of your life, you must learn the best ways to deal with any toxic people. Going forward, you can be polite to them, but be smart and don't let yourself get too close. If you currently have close relationships with toxic people, no matter whom they are, it is time to either part ways totally, or limit your exposure depending on the ties you have with them. If you happen to live, work, or do business with such people, start off by utilizing your resources and form an escape plan first to assure you don't end up in a bad situation. Depending on how crazy or mean these people are, go behind their backs to cut all of the ties you have with them that affect you. These ties can consist of joint bank accounts, same living situations, memberships, projects, jobs, commitments, social events, etc.

Once you have fully cut all of those ties that affect you, and they no longer have any kind of leverage to screw you over, you can then confront them. Remember, you do not have to be rude to them. Never give someone more than they deserve, whether it's good or bad. Just go at it with a very honest, very mature adult approach. You just need to tell them that the friendship, partnership, living situation, work situation, etc. is just not working out and that it is time to move on. No matter how they respond, you need to always respond with "I'm sorry things didn't work out, I wish you the best, and I hope things work out for you." It does not matter how nasty they are to you, if you respond with nothing but kindness and maturity, you make them look bad and yourself look better. Plus, you avoid any legal disputes or conflicts. If you lived with this person, and they refuse to give you your stuff back, all you need to do is call the police, and have a police officer escort you in and out of the house to get your stuff while keeping the peace.

If the people you wish to distance yourself from continue to harass you in anyway, all you need to do is cut them off as soon as possible, and

Do An Overall Analysis Of Your Life

let them know you want nothing to do with them. Do not give them the opportunity to keep hurting you because they may want that. If they call you or text you, block their numbers, if they message you online, block all of their accounts, if they try stalking you at all or harassing you in person, you may go to the police and file a restraining order against them if desperate times call for desperate measures. Don't worry because those are only worst-case scenarios. Usually, the worst thing you will have to do is block them and they will leave you alone. Nobody has the time or the energy to waste on trying to be close to someone who wants nothing to do with them because it is just an unsettling feeling.

Family members, baby mamas, and baby daddies may be a bit of a different story. Some people you have a connection with for certain reasons. In these cases, you need to limit your exposure for your own sake. With family members, you may see them at family gatherings, holiday parties, weddings, funerals, etc. There's nothing wrong with that, as long as nobody mistreats you in anyway. You have no obligation to spend time with any family members who mistreat you or abuse you. It's not fair to you, and you don't deserve it no matter what others tell you.

If you have children with someone, and they happen to be toxic, you need to limit your exposure and only communicate with them if it concerns the kids. Your kids need you, and they are your responsibility, but in order to be the best parent you can be, you need to be the best YOU you can be. No matter what, you control you, so be the better parent and the better person. If they do not want to cooperate, that's on them, not you.

I know that ending some of these relationships can be quite painful at first, but it is just another paradigm shift. Paradigm shifts are like ripping off Band-Aids, the thought can be nerve-racking, actually doing it can be kind of painful, but afterwards, you feel so much better. Once you adjust to life without those people, or without seeing them as often, it becomes a new norm, and you learn to feel much better. So please, once you do that analysis of your life, be sure to remove all of the negative, and make room for the positive. It's kind of like getting rid of the junk you've been hoarding all these years and making room for new stuff. I promise you that things will begin to change after awhile as you let more good into your life.

Remember, as you remove the negatives from your life, you will still need guidance and support from others to heal. As you part ways with toxic people and situations, you must also work on building a healthy support network with the right amount of balance. The diagram below shows you the ideal support network to have and the appropriate amounts of dependency on each.

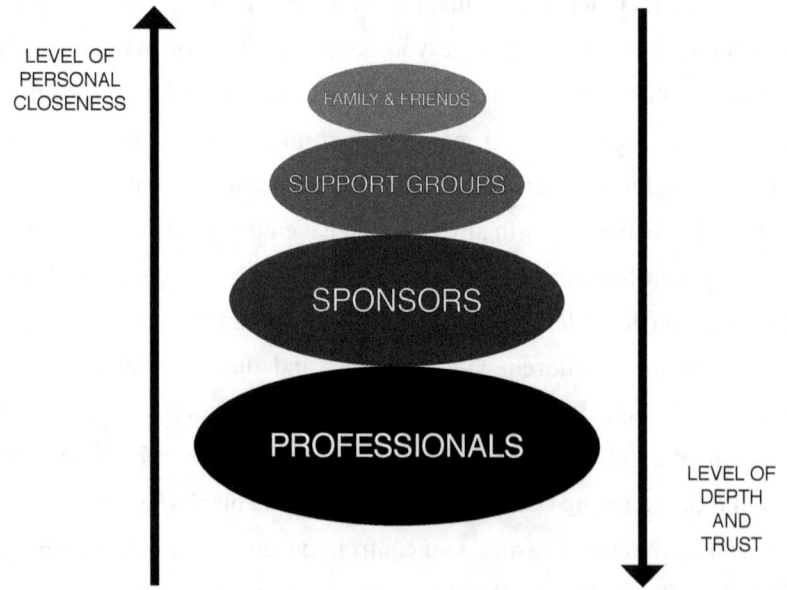

The reason why level of personal closeness and level of depth and trust oppose each other is simply because the closer you are to people, the more biased their opinions could become. Also, personal closeness has the potential to lead to future conflicts. Here are the reasons why each category is where it is.

PROFESSIONALS

The professionals you work with have the lowest level of personal closeness and the highest level of depth and trust. These are the doctors, therapists, counselors, social workers, etc. who are there to carry the majority of your emotional burdens. They can handle it because not only is it their job, but they are highly trained and educated, and they do not have close personal relationships with you. Therefore, their opinions are not biased, and you will be able to hear the truth from them, and be pointed in the right direction. Also, you can tell them anything because due to the Hippocratic oath and certain legal standards, they are obligated to keep everything you tell them confidential. They are there to help you, so by all means, as they gain your trust, be okay with telling them everything. Professionals should make up 40% of your support network.

SPONSORS

As you join fellowships and start your journey to recovery from certain addictions, it is wise for you to get a sponsor. Like I explained in Chapter 11, a sponsor is someone who can walk you through the twelve steps and be there to talk to whenever you need them. A core tradition in any of these fellowships is anonymity, so everyone is expected to abide by that and treat everything as confidential. Your sponsors could be like another therapist in a way, because they will keep your secrets, and they have the wisdom and experience to guide you through your path to recovery. Also, you can develop a closer relationship with them as opposed to a doctor or therapist. They will often give you their phone numbers and invite you to call or text them anytime. Sponsors should make up 30% of your support network.

SUPPORT GROUPS

Joining support groups, such as fellowships, are a great way to make new friends and realize that you are truly not alone. These are good people to talk to about your struggles because chances are, they've had very similar struggles. The best part of these groups is that they are all there for the same reason, and they can all provide each other the support they need to get better. Although they may not have professional level knowledge, they can develop relationships with you that can build into something great. It's okay to share some personal things with them, but your best bet is to keep the most personal things among professionals and sponsors. Support groups should make up 20% of your support network.

FAMILY & FRIENDS

Family and friends are the most important people to have in your life. You want to make sure that they are good for you. Although they are close to you and they love and care about you, their opinions can be the most biased. In other words, they have good intentions, but they may not always know exactly what is best for you and your recovery. Also, if you tell them personal secrets, they are not sworn to secrecy, and they may tell others, especially if they get mad at you over something, and they want to get even. You never want to give them that chance, so the best thing you can do is leave your most personal secrets among professionals and sponsors. If you talk to the right people, they will guide you the right way. Usually, family and friends are there to have a good time, but they are also good to lean on in times of need. Just make sure that they totally earn your trust, but just to be safe, only tell them things you would not mind anyone knowing about you. Realistically, your family and friends should only make up about 10% of your support network, at least when it comes to going too much in depth. Remember that looking for sympathy all the time from family and friends can push them away.

YOUR IDEAL SUPPORT NETWORK

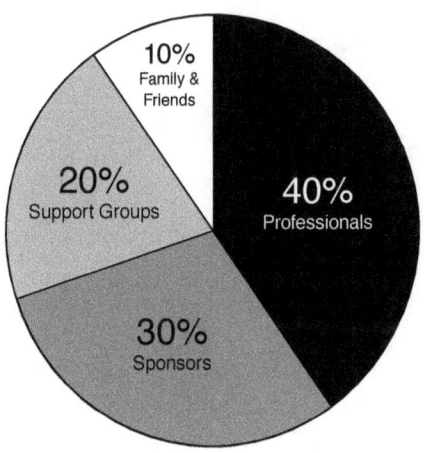

Chapter 13

Start Engaging In Activities That Are Healthy And Fun

As I mentioned in the previous chapter, when you get out of an unhealthy situation, you must give yourself time to adjust, heal, and balance out. It is important that you work on your mental health issues with your therapist, sponsor, fellowship, etc. You need to be proactive and use every resource you need to use because you are worth it. Make time for it, and invest in yourself. Aside from getting the support you need to get better, another way to help speed up your recovery is by engaging in activities that are healthy and fun. Let's face it, if you do nothing but lay around all day, you won't recover as quickly because you will be an object at rest alone with your thoughts. In order to get yourself back in motion, you must give yourself opportunities to relax, have fun, and make new friends.

You might wonder where you can find such activities, or whether or not they will cost you a lot of money. Try your best to find out what you can do either for free or no more than $10 or $20 each time. The most important thing you can start with is figuring out what you enjoy doing, and build off of that with an open mind and the willingness to try different things until you find something that suits you. There are different activities and places you can go for fun all around you. You just need to make the decision to go to Google or Yelp! and find them. The best way to enjoy activities is with other people because being alone all the time can get boring after awhile, but you need a healthy balance between both. You can mix things up by finding hobbies to do when you are alone to keep your mind occupied, and activities you can engage in socially.

The diagram below shows the key motivators that make activities enjoyable:

This diagram displays the four key motivators that actually make activities very enjoyable. The most important one is in the middle because it influences all the other ones. In fact, the influence radiates outward from the inside ones to the outside ones. Here's the break down.

SURVIVAL

Survival is in the center of the diagram because it is the most important motivating factor. Remember that every decision we make is to ensure our survival because that is how our brains are naturally conditioned. Things that make us feel good are perceived as a benefit to our survival, and we have a natural tendency to lean more towards those things.

SOCIAL ACCEPTANCE

Social acceptance comes after survival because survival is the main reason why social acceptance makes us feel good. Like I mentioned earlier, from an evolutionary standpoint, we need to form social bonds to boost our chances of survival. That's why it feels good to make new friends and have others praise us and cheer us on when engaging in activities. The truth is, if we were engaging in a fun activity, but nobody else participated or paid attention, or worse, they booed us and told us that we suck or we did a terrible job, well that would not be fun at all. It would cancel out the two outer layers of the diagram because you would be stressed out and it would hurt your self-esteem. Imagine trying to play a simple game of catch by yourself, or playing with someone who makes fun of you and does not play fair. Would you be having fun? Of course not! Remember that having fun is not always about what you do, it's more about whom you are with. We have fun when we feel good, and we all socialize and encourage each other.

STRESS RELEASE

Stress release comes next because doing something that benefits our survival and allows us to be socially accepted can feel very good. As scary as it sounds, stress can be harmful and even deadly. For that reason, anything that reduces our stress levels makes us feel good. After all, we need that healthy release to prevent it from building up and causing us to explode on someone who may not deserve it. So find your outlet, and go ahead and eliminate that stress because, let's face it, you've earned it!

Chapter 13

SELF-ESTEEM

Self-esteem is boosted as a result of the previous three key factors. Whether it is big or small, it makes us feel good about ourselves. With engaging in healthy activities, we accomplish a few things, we benefit our survival, we form new social bonds to benefit it further, and even better, we reduced our stress levels by finding something we are good at that makes others accept us. This is the best way to begin building self-esteem, especially if yours is very low.

By finding things you enjoy, you find your crowd, or your community. As my saying goes; find your passion, find your community, find yourself. We live in a society now days where people are no longer as close, and we have spread apart into larger areas. As a matter of fact, statistics show that since urbanization and suburbanization, when small, close communities became obsolete, rates of depression increased. That correlation indicates that one of the main causes of depression has to do with a lack of healthy social bonds with others. In today's society, the best way to deal with that is to form your own community, and that can be as simple as a group of friends all engaging in fun activities and enjoying each other's company, or even the fellowships and support groups you join.

Keep in mind that when you are making new friends, they may not understand what you are going through, or they may just want to have a good time and not hear about anybody's problems. When it comes to talking about personal issues, try to keep that among your fellowships, support groups, therapists, etc. Having that balance will help you retain friends and prevent you from scaring them away. As you get closer with certain people, you may be able to open up to them a little more, but give those relationships a chance to grow first.

Chapter 14

Find Ways To Spread Positive Energy

What better way to feel good about yourself and be accepted by others than to give back to your community? Remember when I talked about parasitism versus mutualism? Well, sometimes people who feel as if they are just there for no reason or purpose feel that way because they don't interact with others or contribute to their communities. That feeling of uselessness is mostly caused by internal factors, such as warped perceptions or self-esteem issues. However, the real truth is you will not get noticed if you do nothing about it. Sometimes, all you have to do is just do. Take an opportunity to search around for giving opportunities, such as volunteering at a soup kitchen, donating goods to the needy, or anything that involves helping people who are less fortunate. When you are in a good place, you have the opportunity to be able to help others.

Finding clever ways to help others can boost our chances of survival by gaining social acceptance, making new friends, and even benefitting our survival by making others more likely to help us when we are in need. For example, when I was a kid, my mother used to volunteer at the food pantry in our town, and we donated there all the time. Then, after my parents went through a terrible divorce, we went through a rough financial crisis. When that happened, we could no longer afford to go grocery shopping, so we needed the food pantry, and they were happily there for us in our time of need. That is how mutualistic people work. If you help them, they will help you. Those are the kinds of relationships you want to build. Just remember that you need to have a healthy balance between giving to others and giving to yourself.

If you do not have a whole lot of time in your life to volunteer, that's okay. You can find clever ways to do little things throughout each day when they come to you. Little things include holding the door for someone, giving compliments, helping someone with minor issues that you could solve easily, donating an extra $1 to $5 to a local charity or organization when asked by the cashier at checkout, buying a stranger a cup of coffee, helping people clean up when possible, or even making a simple phone call to a friend who is having a hard time. One thing I learned in life is that I can do things that take little to no effort on my part, but they can have a major positive impact on the person or people on the receiving end. You never know how much something so little to you can mean to someone else. After all, it's all about perception.

Although the purpose of healing is to help yourself first, helping others along the way is a great way to make you feel good about yourself. Once you begin to feel good about yourself, it will help you change your mindset to a more positive one, and with a positive mindset, you can start having better thoughts. Remember that our thoughts emit frequencies out into the universe, and due to resonance, the frequencies we emit will attract like frequencies in the universe. Therefore, what you put out into the universe is what will come back. If you would like to learn more about this phenomenon, I highly recommend reading the book *The Secret* by Rhonda Byrne.

I know positive thinking can be a very difficult thing to do when you have been stuck in a negative mindset for so long. The truth is, not everyone knows how to get out of those patterns. This is why we must take action in our lives to figure out what external factors are keeping us in our negative states of mind. By finding a way to get the ball rolling, reaching out for help, doing an overall life analysis, and looking for fun activities to do, we really begin to change our overall perceptions on life and realize that there is much more to it than what we know. Let's refer to the diagram on the next page...

Find Ways To Spread Positive Energy

YOU

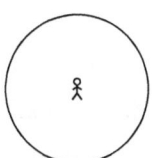

EVERYTHING YOU'VE EXPERIENCED IN LIFE SO FAR

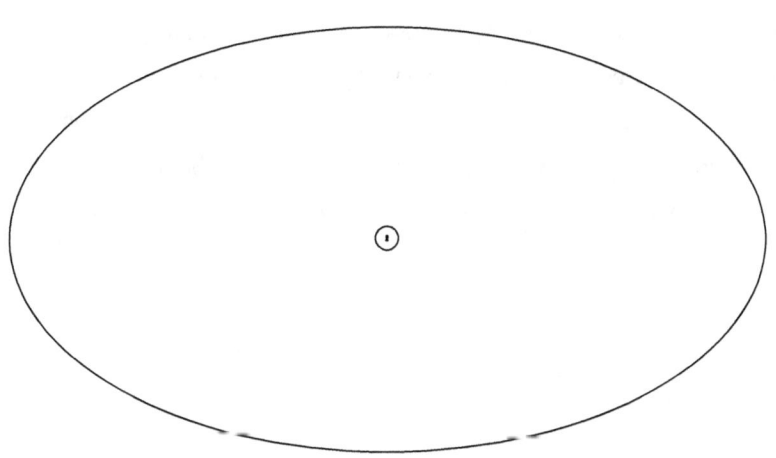

EVERYTHING ELSE OUT THERE

With that visualization, you should now understand that there really is more to life than what you know. No matter how intelligent you are, you must be willing to accept the fact that there are things you don't know, and by accepting that, you can get excited about learning new things. Once you get in motion towards the right direction you wish to go in, your mood and your outlook on life will change. When you allow yourself to discover other ways of life as opposed to what you know, you can really make a positive change. The best place to start, for now, is by looking for ways to spread positive energy because this will open new doors for you and give you good feelings.

Remember that all humans have that Jekyll and Hyde complex. In other words, we all naturally have empathy and sympathy, but our fight or flight responses can disable them. Removing any negatives from your life will make you no longer constantly need your fight or flight mechanisms, which will allow you the chance to have empathy and sympathy, and will make you want to help others. Of course, we need those fight or flight mechanisms for emergency situations, but that is what they are truly meant for, emergencies. So, without constantly being in unhealthy situations that have you on edge all the time, you can make better decisions and feel good about helping others. I believe in the idea of being the person who was not there for me, so go out and do good things. I promise you it will be worthwhile.

Chapter 15

Build Your Career & Your Self-Esteem

Many people struggle with self-esteem issues. I definitely struggled with those issues my whole life. It affects more people than you think, but there is a way to turn things around to avoid problems in the future. There were many things I tried that just did not do it for me such as therapy, hospitalization, partial hospital programs, hanging out with certain people, etc. Although all of those factors contributed to my better health and well–being, what really helped me get the ball rolling was discovering my true passions in life and pursuing a career doing something I loved. It took some time and some failures to figure it all out, but I found my happiness in entrepreneurship, and I knew that I needed to pursue it to be happy. I began feeling the feelings of being successful and having what I want in life, and I've been working towards it ever since.

Basically, when it comes to true happiness and success, along with higher self-esteem, there are four keys to it:

1. *Having a healthy mind, body, and soul*
2. *Doing something you absolutely love*
3. *Making a living off of it*
4. *Having positive relationships with others*

There is a synergy among the four because they are all necessary to balance you out. Please refer to the diagram on the next page.

Chapter 15

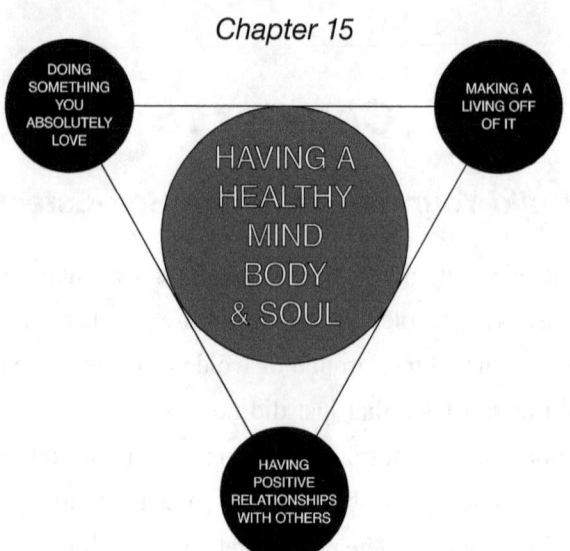

HAVING A HEALTHY MIND, BODY, & SOUL

Having a healthy mind, body, and soul are essential to living a happy life. Of course, you definitely need those other three keys to achieve it, but in order to be truly happy and fulfilled in life, you must learn how to find happiness within yourself. Many people in the world have success, money, family, etc., but they are unhappy because they have not fully satisfied themselves in life.

Although giving to others can nourish our souls, we also need to tend to our own needs and find the healthy balance between helping ourselves and helping others. This is why the beginning of your journey should consist of taking care of any issues you have first, or at least start making an effort towards it. You must utilize as many resources as you need and use them to analyze your life and remove the negatives. After all, if you start building on a weak foundation, your house will eventually collapse. Once you begin uncovering the roots of your underlying issues and spiritual emptiness, you will be able to build a stronger foundation on which you can build anything.

DOING SOMETHING YOU ABSOLUTELY LOVE

Let's face it, we all need to work in order to make money and pay our bills, and life is too short to do something that does not fully satisfy us. Some might think that not working at all would be the best thing ever, but in reality, it can make you depressed and, eventually, complacent. You begin to feel useless and it only hurts your self-esteem more. After all, you can only watch so much Netflix before you start getting bored. On the other hand, if you do something you either do not enjoy or you hate, you will not be happy no matter how much money you make. In order to be truly successful, you must do something you enjoy, feel good about, and even feel a sense of pride for. If you do not feel that sense of pride, or even worse, if you feel that what your doing is immoral, unethical, or even illegal, that guilt and paranoia will build up and hurt you. Much like activities, jobs have similar key motivators that make them enjoyable:

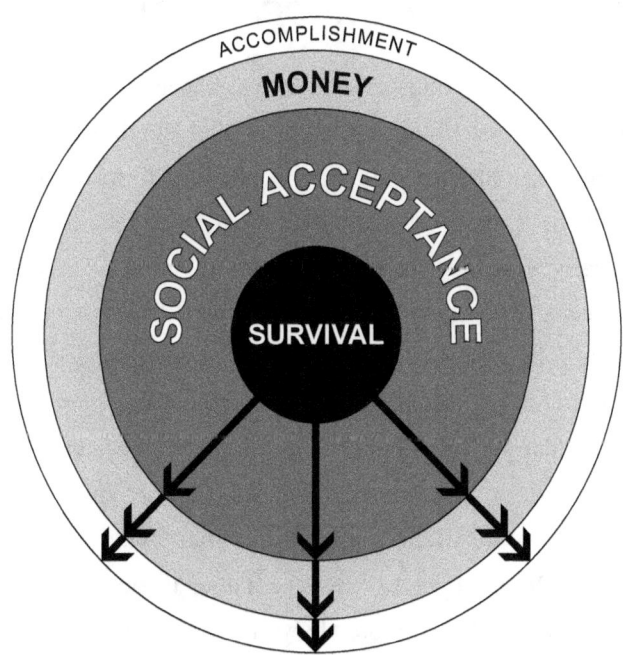

The diagram on the previous page displays the four key motivators that actually make jobs very enjoyable. The most important one is in the middle because it influences all the other ones. Once again, the influence radiates outward from the inside ones to the outside ones.

SURVIVAL

Survival is in the center of this diagram as well because it is the most important motivating factor. Remember that every decision we make is to ensure our survival because that is how our brains are conditioned, and we need to make money to survive. Things that make us feel good, like earning income, are perceived as a benefit to our survival, and we have a natural tendency to lean more towards those things.

SOCIAL ACCEPTANCE

Social acceptance comes after survival because survival is the main reason why social acceptance makes us feel good. Like I mentioned earlier, from an evolutionary standpoint, we need to form social bonds to boost our chances of survival. That's why it feels good to build positive relationships with clients, coworkers, bosses, managers, etc. When we find a job or career path that we love, and we constantly advance and impress others, especially those more experienced than us, it makes us feel great.

Wouldn't you feel amazing if you worked hard on a project, and your boss told you that you did a fantastic job, and even gave you a raise? How about if you earned a promotion, and all of your coworkers threw an office party for you? An environment like that would make almost any job enjoyable. On the flip side, how much does it suck to get yelled at by your boss? Or disliked and ignored by your coworkers? I have experienced that in the past, and it made me dread going to work. As you can see, that is why social acceptance is one of the most important key motivators to job satisfaction; especially when you receive opportunities for career advancement.

MONEY

Although money is necessary for paying our bills, getting through life, and is the main reason why we work, it is not the biggest motivator. The truth is, money is not always enough to motivate a person. They say that money does not buy happiness, and there is a lot of truth to that. In fact, according to Mitchell Moffit and Gregory Brown from ASAPScience on YouTube, studies show that when people make $75,000 a year or more, the level of happiness is not impacted. It's the main reason why we work, and it allows us to survive both biologically and economically, but it does not always give us that drive we need or that feeling of excitement about it. What we really get excited about is the interactions we have with others.

ACCOMPLISHMENT

When we complete tasks that we enjoy, make money doing it, and gain the acceptance of others, it allows us to feel a sense of accomplishment. We feel good about doing something we are good at, serving others, and, of course, earning that paycheck. Besides, what makes us feel good about going home afterwards to relax is the fact that we worked hard to earn that time to just settle down, and we did something to benefit our survival.

If you can come up with your ideal career path, no matter what it is, I encourage you to turn that vision into a reality. It takes a lot of hard work, but it will be totally worth it in the end. There are many people out there, who may doubt you, but that happens to everyone. You just need to learn to accept it and not listen to them. The truth is, no matter what anyone says, anyone is capable of accomplishing anything. The key is to be willing to do whatever it takes to get there, legally and ethically of course, and you must be able to accept the reality of the situation. If you cannot accept the reality of that career path, it may not be ideal for you, and you should choose something else.

When working hard to get to where you need to be, it may be a bit of a struggle, but that is how success works. Just learn to take it one day at a time, and do not be afraid to rely on your support network. One of my methods to getting through college and having to work a job at the same time is to allow myself to have fun at least once a week. In fact, I once had a professor who went back to school in his 40s, and he told our class that he worked 40 hours a week while taking 6 courses at a time. Even though he took on a lot at once, he told us that him and his wife would go out dancing every Friday night to ease that stress. That really stuck with me, and I learned to allow myself to have fun at least once a week when I have a lot going on. So go out there, find what you truly want to do in life, and do whatever it takes to get there. Embrace the journey, and cherish the end result.

MAKING A LIVING OFF OF IT

What else would be better than doing what you enjoy doing than getting paid for it at the same time? Not just getting paid, but getting paid a living wage in which you can live off of independently if needed. You may have heard a lot of hype from successful people about getting rich and living your dream life. Although that is possible with hard work and dedication, the truth is, you do not need incredible wealth to be happy and successful, all you need is financial security, financial stability, and at the very most, financial freedom. All you really need in life is enough money to pay for all of the things you need and most of the things you want. Any more than that is extra. So, if you wish to be truly successful in life, don't feel like you need to put too much pressure on yourself to become the next millionaire or billionaire. If you want to, then, by all means, go for it, but if not, it's okay.

Often times, you will hear people say that you need to spend money to make money, and that is true because everything involves investment. Whether you are an entrepreneur investing money into starting your own business, or a college student paying tuition to earn a degree and get a good paying job, it always comes with a price. What you get in return, however, is totally worth it. The key is not to overwhelm yourself by taking on more than you can handle. You do not want to have to spend more than you earn.

The key here is having a healthy balance between income and expenses. Ideally, you would like your income to outweigh your expenses, so you have extra. However, all you need to do to survive is break even. The amount of income you have left after expenses, such as bills, taxes, mortgages, etc., are paid is known as disposable personal income (DPI), which you can either spend or save. This is the money that should go towards the things you want whether you will get them in the present or in the future. I believe that true wealth should be based on your DPI, or what you have left over.

Let's say you are a 16-year-old kid in high school, who works a minimum wage job averaging $200 per week. If your parents pay all of your expenses, and you have no responsibilities, your entire paycheck is your disposable income. Now, let's say you are a 45-year-old CEO of a large company averaging $350 million each year. That's a lot of money, right? However, you have many extravagant assets such as a big mansion, 5 Lamborghini's, 2 Roll's Royce's, 3 summer homes, a spouse and 6 children, along with maids, butlers, landscapers, nannies, etc. The majority of your income goes towards all of these expenses, leaving you with an average of $200 per week left over in spending money. When it comes to DPI, you are on the same level as that 16-year-old.

Chapter 15

The key to financial balance is learning how to differentiate properly between necessities and desires. You need food, water, shelter, clothing, a car, etc., but do you really need 5 Lamborghini's and 2 Roll's Royce's? In marketing, they talk about the difference between functional needs and psychological needs. Psychologically, you may desire a Lamborghini or a Roll's Royce, but when it comes to functionality, a Honda Civic or a Toyota Camry will do the same thing with more reliability, more fuel efficiency, and a lot less money. No matter how wealthy you might be, your best bet is to always live within or less than your means. After all, when you save as much as you can, you can use that money to secure yourself and your family financially, save it for emergencies, or let it build up and put it towards something great.

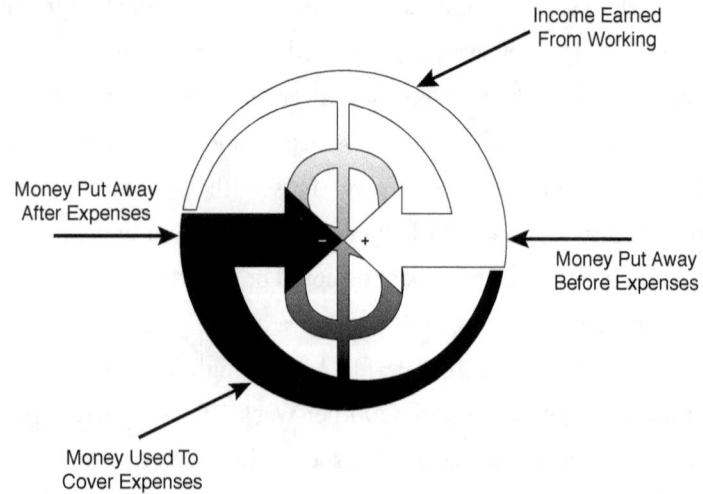

In the diagram I created above, I visually represented a money saving method I developed years ago. Of course, sometimes life happens, and necessities become expensive, but for the most part, I stick to this method. I used this method to get out of a minimum wage job I hated. I spent months living dirt broke until I saved up enough money for a down payment on a brand new car. That car was an investment, and I used it to become an Uber driver, so I could make better money, be my own boss, and leave the job that was not working out for me. Every investment I make is a stepping-stone towards a greater version of myself.

When it comes to saving money and having that financial security, you must figure out your average weekly or monthly income and your expenses. If you need help, you may consult with an accountant or any kind of financial advisor, but you could also roughly estimate. One method I always used over the years was tricking myself into thinking I earned less than I really did, and that mentality helped me save a lot of money. Another budgeting technique I used depended on my paychecks; if I made between $100 and $200 in a week, I would save $100 and keep the rest, but if I made more than $200, I would keep $100 and save the rest. Again, I know it is tough when you have expenses, but getting in that routine will benefit you long-term when you need to invest in yourself or have that extra cushion in the bank.

So, keep in mind that you do not need to be filthy rich to be truly successful, all you need is a career you enjoy that pays you enough money to live comfortably and happily. After all, like I mentioned earlier, money alone will not buy happiness.

HAVING POSITIVE RELATIONSHIPS WITH OTHERS

This is by far the most important factor to being truly happy and successful in life. Although you need money to have a healthy social life, having nothing but that money will not make it worthwhile without friends and family. Like I mentioned in Chapter 3, we all depend on each other for survival because there are certain tasks that are too much for one to take on. This is why being lonely can make us depressed, angry, and even insane because that is our brain's way of letting us know that our survival is being threatened and we need to do something about it. Positive social bonds are the core essence of true happiness, and we depend on them very much. Let's face it, if you had the best, highest paying job in the world, and you earned more money than most could ever imagine, but you had no friends or family, you would not be happy. If you are not happy, it will affect your job and every other aspect of your life. It is crucial to understand the different types of social bonds we have in life.

PROFESSIONAL RELATIONSHIPS

These types of relationships are good, but they have the least amount of intimacy. These are the connections you have with co-workers, clients, bosses, managers, doctors, therapists, dentists, etc. You confide in these relationships either as the receiver or the giver. The giver is the one who provides the product or service and earns money, and the receiver receives the product or service and spends money. We rely on our employers or our clients to pay us money, and we build relationships with them to make them feel valuable to us, which displays mutual respect. Although you help each other in that way, it does not always mean you could be compatible as friends or more. In fact, in most cases, getting too close with these people could be looked at as unethical or inappropriate.

FAMILY

They say family comes first, and that it is the most important social bond to have. The truth is, however, we should only prioritize family if they treat us with the same respect. You see, a normal and healthy family is supposed to provide unconditional love and support to each other, but it does not always work out that way. Like I mentioned in Chapter 8, we have no control over the families we are born into, and we often grow up being a lot like them because they influence us the most. Unless, of course, we gain an outside perspective on life that changes our ways of thinking.

However, once we grow up, and we are able to financially support ourselves, we have a choice of whether or not we want to continue associating with the families we are born into. Of course, if they are loving, supportive, and normal, for the most part, they are an absolute blessing. On the flipside, if they are toxic, abusive, controlling, or unhealthy in any way, we must keep a safe distance, no matter how much it hurts. After all, once we find love and settle down to start our own families, that's when we have control, and we can choose to learn from our parents' mistakes.

FRIENDS

Many people say that friends are the family we choose, and I believe in that myself. We do have control in the friends we make, and friends are one of the most wonderful assets in life. We just need to make sure that they are healthy for us to be around. For most of my life, I made the mistake of being friends with people who I was not compatible with, and it either did not work out or I was betrayed. Either way, it taught me a lot. The basic foundation of a friendship involves mutual trust, mutual respect, and mutual loyalty because good friends should have your back no matter what. I used to believe it was that simple, but I was wrong. Aside from trust, respect, and loyalty, you also need to have common grounds.

When it comes to having friends, especially your close ones, you want to make sure you are both in similar places and going the same direction in life because healthy friendships are supposed to be mutually beneficial, which means that most people should be able to benefit off each other equally. I know to some, this may sound selfish, but remember that you need to look out for yourself first. As you discover your passions and pursue your ideal career, you will start meeting new people who have those common interests and goals. You may lose some of the friends you had, but that is natural and more common than you think. No matter what, all you need to do when friends come and go is wish them well in life.

PYRAMID OF SUCCESSFUL FRIENDSHIPS

LOVE & RELATIONSHIPS

They say there is someone for everyone, and everyone needs someone. Naturally we fall in love in order to mate and pass on our genes. It is a survival mechanism, and it is meant to keep people together, so they can raise offspring together. The modern world is different, and many people do not fully understand what love is supposed to be, which is why you must learn to be satisfied with yourself first. Just like with friends, you will meet the person most compatible for you once you become the best version of yourself, which involves doing what you love and being in an ideal place. Remember that like attracts like, and in order to be with the ideal person, you need to be ideal for them as well.

PYRAMID OF SUCCESSFUL RELATIONSHIPS

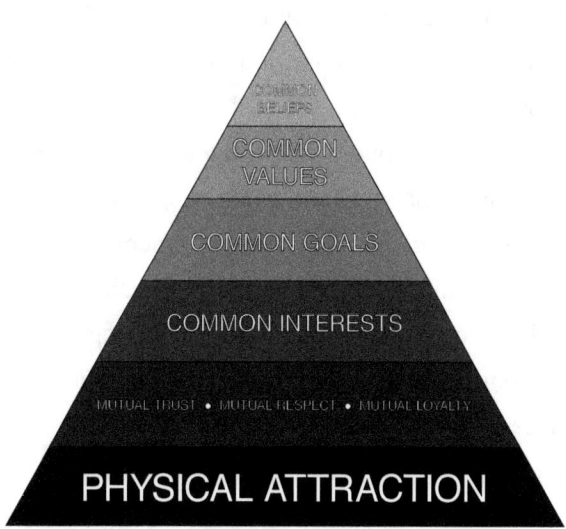

As you can see, the pyramid of successful relationships is almost exactly like the pyramid of successful friendships. However, in this one, the bottom of the pyramid, and the initial part, is the physical attraction towards one another. Now, I know that may sound shallow, but according to Laci Green from *D News*, the first stage of love is lust. Let's face it, what is the first thought in a typical guy's head when he sees an attractive woman? Come on guys, back me up on this. You would say to yourself, "I'd tap that," right? As opposed to saying, "I'd take 'that' out to dinner," or "I'd get to know 'that'." Not to be degrading in any way, but it is true, and I believe women have a similar mentality when they see an attractive man. It is only natural, and you could feel that way towards anyone you find physically attractive. It is very important to be physically attracted to your partner, especially when you get intimate, because if you are not, they will find out, and it will do more harm than good.

Aside from the physical attraction, in order to have a successful relationship, the two must build that foundation of mutual trust, respect, and loyalty, without any of that, you will have a failed relationship. At one point, I believed that being nice and loyal to one another was enough, but again, I was wrong. In addition to all of that, like with friends, you also need to have those common grounds (interests, goals, values, and beliefs). Although you need to be mutual and have things in common, you also need to have some opposing attributes. They say opposites attract, and the truth to that is having certain opposing attributes, as long as they are positive, will allow two people to complement each other, or balance each other out. It's kind of like how running a business requires different people with different skill sets who have common goals. Let's face it, if everyone in a company only knew how to be accountants, you would have a failed business.

If you are currently in a relationship that is unhealthy, or simply just not working out, do not be afraid to end it. As much as it may hurt to be heart broken, you can always move passed it and find someone new. In order to be ready for a new relationship, you must give your heart time to heal, and give yourself a chance to move on from the feelings you had for the previous person. If you do not give yourself time to move on, you will most likely end up bringing your issues from your previous relationship into your new relationship, and that is never a good thing. So remember, never settle for less, and always strive for better. No matter what, if things do not work out, and that person is nasty to you, simply just wish them well and move on.

The last misconception about relationships I would like to point out is the dilemma of "whose fault is it that it did not work out?" There are many people out there who often either blame themselves or blame the other person for their issues. I used to always blame myself when things went wrong because I had low self-esteem. However, the truth is that in a relationship, each person only has 50% control. Therefore, you can only control you, and not the other person. If both people in a relationship are willing to put 100% into their 50%, it has the potential to be a successful relationship. Otherwise, it just will not work out.

I apologize for such a lengthy chapter. I promise you that these are my final thoughts for it. When you consider your overall relationships with others, you need to prioritize them properly. I know society is accustomed to certain norms and phrases such as "family comes first", "blood is thicker than water", or even "bros before hoes," but the truth is, you need to prioritize people based on how they treat you. No matter who they are, how close they are to you, how long you've known each other, or whether or not they are related to you, the ones who treat you best should be on the top of that list.

Let's use "bros before hoes", for example, if you are a guy who has good guy friends who treat you well and have your back no matter what, but you are with a girl who does not treat you right, obviously you will prioritize your guy friends. Now, let's flip it; let's say you are in a healthy relationship with a girl who treats you well, loves you, cares for you, has your back, and would do anything for you, but your guy friends are all jerks to you. Who will you prioritize there? Obviously, the girlfriend would be the right choice, but many guys believe that their buddies need to come before their girlfriends no matter what. That is wrong. In addition to that, let's say you have good friends and a good girlfriend or boyfriend, but your family treats you badly. Does family come first in this scenario? The answer is no, and that is difficult for many people to comprehend because of what society makes us believe.

No matter what, go with your gut, and if you feel like people are mistreating you, do not let them do that. Always be sure to prioritize the ones who have your back and make you feel good about yourself. Like I mentioned in Chapter 12, you must part ways with toxic people and begin to build a strong support network. That foundation will allow you to branch out and form the right social bonds with the people you encounter on your journey to happiness and success.

Chapter 16

The Power Of Forgiveness

You are probably wondering why forgiveness should come later in your journey. Well the truth is, as you work through your struggles and your pain, you learn to forgive, but it is difficult to do so sometimes. In fact, forgiveness can be one of the most difficult things to do, but it is essential to your recovery and your overall happiness and success. Holding onto grudges, anger, resentment, guilt, lies, etc. tends to weigh you down and get heavier as time goes on. You cannot truly move on in life without lightening that load, and the only way to lighten it is by forgiving both yourself and others.

FORGIVING YOURSELF

As we grow up and go through life, we make mistakes, and we either learn from them or repeat them. Sometimes, especially when we have low self-esteem, we can be really hard on ourselves for making these mistakes, no matter how small they are. The important thing to understand here is that everyone makes similar mistakes growing up. In reality, it is nothing other than a learning process. This is why it is necessary for us to seek professional help and really analyze our lives and ourselves. If you can gain an outside perspective to clarify your perception of reality, you will be more aware of your actions, and you will make fewer mistakes in the future. Once you have the correct sense of right and wrong, you can focus on always doing the right thing, which is what we should be doing anyway.

Forgiving yourself can be one of the most difficult tasks you will ever face, but the best place to start is with positive self-talk. You need to remind yourself that you are only human, making mistakes is all part of growing up and learning, and it is never too late to do the right thing; remember how people work on a logical and biological level. Plus, the fact that it is never a person's fault when they end up a certain way, but eventually it becomes their responsibility to do something about it. Once you realize that, all you need to do is take action and do something about it.

If you choose to join a fellowship and do a twelve step program, you will see that steps 8 & 9 involve making a list of all persons you had harmed and then going out to make direct amends to them all. When you do that, especially after a fair amount of time has passed, you will learn that most people have moved on and they have no problem forgiving you, especially if you give them sincere apologies. Just make sure you do this properly with the help of your sponsor. Keep in mind that not everyone will forgive you, and if some people refuse to forgive you, it is not a poor reflection of your character; it is a poor reflection of theirs'. Remember, most people who have very warped perceptions can take things too personally, so what you did may not be as bad as you or they might think.

In addition, if someone you wronged tries to convince you that you "owe them", and they are trying to use guilt to manipulate you into doing what they want, putting you down, hurting you, or violating you in any way, that is them being negative and seeking out revenge. No matter what you did to them, the punishment never fits the crime, and you do not deserve to be mistreated by anyone you have wronged. Unfortunately, people with low self-esteem tend to feel like they deserve some kind of punishment, so they put up with unfair treatment. The best thing you can do in this situation is analyze it with a professional or an experienced person you can trust, and you may realize that you are being abused for no reason at all, other than the fact that the person doing it has some sick and twisted revenge fantasies. If it makes you feel better, just give them a sincere apology and admit that you were wrong because that's all you can do in that situation; if people refuse to forgive you, that has nothing to do with you, and it's due to their personal issues. Simply just move on, and remind yourself that you made an honest mistake, and it will never happen again. Wish them well, and go separate ways.

FORGIVING OTHERS

Forgiving others can be tough due to many conflicts and misunderstandings in life, and we encounter a lot of people who hurt us. Some of these situations we can just brush off, but others impact us deeply. The first step to forgiveness is removing yourself from the unhealthy social interaction or situation because if someone is continually hurting you, it will only fuel your resentment towards them and keep you adapted to a toxic environment. That's why you must part ways in order to adapt to a healthier environment and balance out. Once you part ways, you must allow yourself time to feel and to heal, and find any of the resources discussed in Chapter 11 to be able to work through the pain.

Once you start processing what was done to you and you handle the pain, you can begin to think rationally again and learn more about the situation. When people hurt us, all we see are the mean things they do, but what we do not see is what they went through to become the way they are. Once you can understand and sympathize with people who have wronged you, it will become easier to let go of the resentment and forgive. You may start forgiving as soon as you are ready, no matter where you are in your journey. However, you may not be able to forgive fully until you are in a better place yourself, and you are either no longer affected by what was done to you, or something positive came out of it. Once you are in a better place, certain incidents from the past will most likely not mean anything to you anymore. You may choose to forgive certain people directly or indirectly depending on the situation. Directly involves confrontation, and indirectly involves no confrontation, but you just let go of the resentment on your own.

When forgiving those who hurt you, you must understand the difference between forgiving people and trusting them again. Keep in mind that most people do not change, and it is not because they cannot change, it is because they either do not know how to, or they do not want to. Unfortunately, that is out of your control, and it is up to them whether or not they want the help. Often times, people need to hit rock bottom before they decide to make a positive change, but sadly, not everyone is willing to put their pride aside. Remember, you cannot control other people; you can only control yourself, and with that being said, focus on what you can do and find your inner peace.

In most cases, when you forgive someone, you do not want to rekindle any kind of relationship with that person. Even though forgiveness is healthy, some people may not be willing to discontinue their negative behavior, so being around them will still be unhealthy. No matter what, you do not want to give people who have wronged you in the past more opportunities to wrong you again because it will be just like starting over with more resentment. On the other hand, if you forgive people who are willing to do whatever it takes to change for the better, treat you with respect, and rectify the situation, it is possible to rekindle a relationship as long as you can both move passed what happened. In these cases, you need to be cautious, and you need to make those people prove themselves worthy to you. After all, nothing is worth you getting hurt all over again. So, whether or not you choose to rebuild broken relationships, always forgive and wish people the best no matter what. By doing that, you will prove to others that you are the bigger person, and no matter how the people you forgive act or react, nobody can take that away from you.

Chapter 17

Maintaining A Balanced Life

Once you get to a certain point in your life, and you have overcome the majority of your struggles, you will begin to attract greater things as you grow. Remember, everything is about balance and moderation, so too much of anything can be bad. You will not have unlimited happiness in only one aspect of your life because it does not work that way. However, if you maintain a balance among these 7 major aspects of life, you will be in a good place.

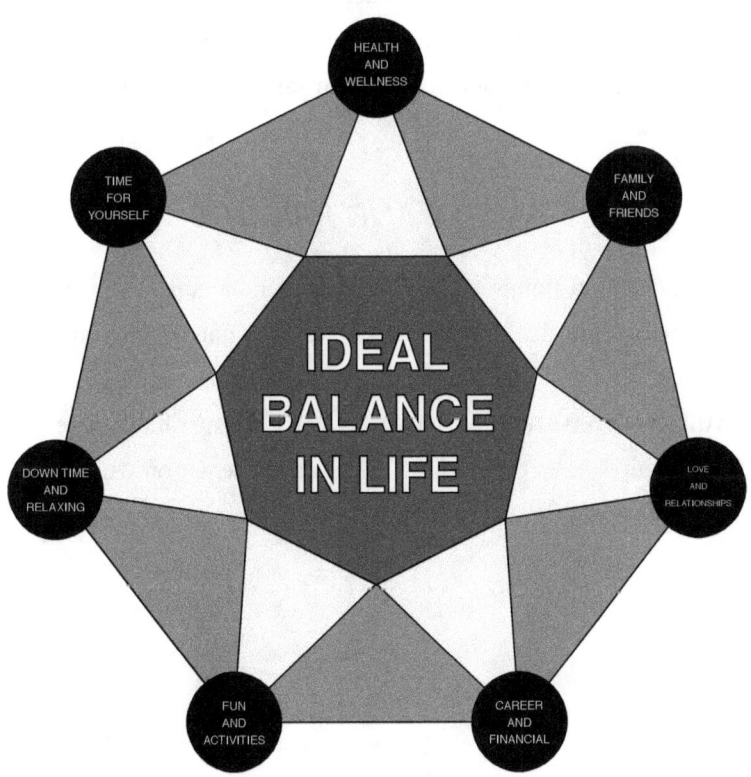

Chapter 17

HEALTH AND WELLNESS

Health and wellness are the most important components to your happiness and well-being. Although you need all of the others to truly have it, it is your foundation. Let's face it, when you are not healthy or well, your stress levels go up, your happiness declines, and your work and relationships can suffer big time. There are certain times in our lives when we may not have time to go to the gym, or we cannot afford to eat healthy because it is too expensive. Here's a little secret; when you spend a little extra money on healthier foods, you will spend less money on medical bills in the long run. The key is to get yourself in the ideal financial situation where you do not need to work ridiculous hours just to make ends meet. This is why it is crucial to go after your ideal career path because then, you will be able to do what you love, make good money, and have that extra time for yourself and your family and friends.

FAMILY AND FRIENDS

Positive social bonds are essential to our mental health, which can also affect our physical health. Since we all want some form of social acceptance, we need to make sure that we go after the right forms of it that will benefit us on our journey. The people we surround ourselves with most frequently have the highest levels of influence on us. Refer to the image on the next page...

OUR SURVIVAL

GREATEST THREAT		GREATEST BENEFIT
SURROUNDED BY NEGATIVE PEOPLE	ALONE	SURROUNDED BY POSITIVE PEOPLE

When people surround us, being around mostly negative people is the greatest threat to our survival, and being around mostly positive people is the greatest benefit. Being alone, on the other hand, is the gray area because we have nobody to hurt us, but also, nobody to help and support us. This is why it is so important to begin the process of what I call Social Detoxing, which is when you remove the negative people out of your life and make room for the positive. It takes some time to adapt to this change, so do not be concerned if there are little to no immediate results. Just take it slowly, or one day at a time. If everyone learned to remove those toxic people from their lives, and nobody helped them anymore, they would have no choice but to reach out for help to the proper resources, and start their own journeys with me or anyone else. If you have been losing a lot of good people in your life, and you realize you are a toxic person, do not be alarmed. Simply just accept it and find the resources to help you improve yourself, and greater things will come.

The best way to deal with anyone is to always start off with the willingness to cooperate and be respectful. If the other people respond with the same respect and cooperation, you can build healthy relationships with them. However, if they respond to your kindness with rudeness and aggression, simply just wish them well and do not pursue any kind of connections with them. The key here is not to take things personally because many of us often internalize the behaviors of other people, but the truth is you cannot control them, and they are that way for reasons that have nothing to do with you.

The kind of balance you need here is a balance between kindness and assertiveness. You must always start with kindness, but then conform and adapt to how the other person is acting. This is an effective technique often used in negotiations in order to come to a fair deal when one party is not being very fair. So, when it comes to family and friends, have fun, laugh, enjoy life, do not let others walk all over you, and just keep those negative individuals at a safe distance.

LOVE AND RELATIONSHIPS

Finding love is meant to be one of the greatest feelings in the world because, on a biological basis, we need to attract our ideal mates to pass on our genes. Aside from reproduction, we need to have a partner, who we can trust, feel safe with, connect with, show affection to, and ultimately, have a healthy sex life with. Even though sex is only one part of a healthy relationship, it is the most intimate you can get with a person, and it has many health benefits such as reduced anxiety, improved memory, higher self-esteem, healthy levels of oxytocin, etc.

Unfortunately, many people are robbed of the good feelings love is supposed to bring because they end up with the wrong person. In more extreme cases, people are abused, raped, beaten, sexually addicted, cheated on, neglected, etc. In less extreme cases, certain people just lack the common grounds and complementary attributes they need to have a successful relationship, and because they have feelings or have a fear of hurting the other person's feelings, they stay with that person. Having feelings for the wrong people can be painful, especially if they are hurting you in anyway. When looking for the right person to be with, refer back to the Pyramid of Successful Relationships from Chapter 15, and make sure to establish everything in the pyramid from the bottom level up. You ever hear people tell you to "take things slow"? Well, this is exactly why because you want to make sure you can establish everything from the physical attraction, to the mutual trust, respect, and loyalty, and then the common grounds and complementary attributes.

CAREER AND FINANCIAL

Although having a successful career and sustainable income is necessary for our economic survival, it is unhealthy to make your whole life about it. Of course, you need to find a career path that can fulfill you and support you financially, but you still need to have time for family and friends. Like I mentioned in Chapter 15, in order for anything in life to fulfill you, you must have positive relationships with the people you work with, and with your friends and family. I believe the ideal life would be having a career you love, so you can look forward to going to work every day. Then, after a long day of work, you can look forward to coming home to a loving family or good friends. It takes a lot of hard work to get to this point, but once you do, and you start a family of your own, allow yourself to have that healthy balance and give yourself things to look forward to every day.

FUN AND ACTIVITIES

Much like having an ideal career, it is also important to have enjoyable activities to do with others. Having a career to financially support these activities is key, especially a career that also allows you the time to do so. Have you ever thought of any kinds of leisure activities that you might enjoy? Well, now would be a good time to see if there are any of those activities near you. Whether you like to sing, dance, go to the movies, play sports, socialize, go out to eat, etc., life is too short not to do those things, and by doing those things, you allow yourself to exert that built up energy inside you and relieve some stress. After all, we all need our outlets.

DOWN TIME AND RELAXING

There are plenty of ways to be productive and have fun, but what better way to recharge yourself and prepare for them than to have down time? Whether it is sleeping, cuddling, watching Netflix, eating, etc., it is necessary to have time to unwind, so you can recuperate. After all, our bodies need fuel and rest in order to keep going. Again, just like everything else, you need to have a healthy balance between downtime and activity because too much activity can physically exhaust you to the point where you can damage yourself, and too much downtime can make you complacent and increase chances of obesity, diseases, not enough circulation or exercise, etc. So, after a hard day's work or a fun time out with friends, end the day with a nice way to relax and recharge. After all, you've earned it!

TIME FOR YOURSELF

They say loneliness is unhealthy, and selfishness will get you nowhere, but believe it or not, to some degree, you need to be selfish. I am not saying become an arrogant person who cares only about him/herself, but you need to truly figure out what you want or need in life, and go after it. We all need to give to others in order to be happy in life, but we also must give to ourselves and have that healthy balance. It is critical to go after what you truly want in life because you do not want to regret missing out on opportunities later in life. No matter what, if you have good people in your life, they will be happy for you and support whatever you want to do. However, if people do not support you, and they feel entitled to be in your life when they are not helping you grow, they are the ones being truly selfish.

The truth is, we all need our personal space at times because it is unhealthy to be joined at the hip with others 24/7. I admit I was guilty of being too clingy in past relationships, but I learned later on that I was overcompensating for being starved of affection most of my life. On the flip side, I realized that if I am with a woman who does not want to be touched or intimate at all, that does not work for me. The point here is never to settle for less than you deserve, especially when it comes to the people in your life. If you have friends or relationships that hold you back from your goals in life, you must cut ties with them. As painful as it is, you will meet better people who are more compatible with you as you venture through your journey.

For example, if your goal is to get sober from drugs or alcohol, you can no longer hang around with the friends you used to drink or use with. Likewise, if you wish to be successful in life, you must be willing to surround yourself with other successful people, and not let others hold you back. There is a common misconception about successful people screwing over or betraying their old friends, but the truth is those old friends may not have been what was best for them. By surrounding themselves with the old friends, they remain on their level, but by surrounding themselves with other successful people, they can level up. One issue that people with low self-esteem have is that they like to surround themselves with people beneath them to make them feel better in contrast, but by doing that, they remain on that same lower level. When you surround yourself with people who are more experienced, wealthier, and more successful than you, you can learn from them and get up onto their level. Imagine you are climbing a mountain, and you have people below you and people above you; who will be able to give you a hand to get to the top? The ones above you!

The key to ending relationships with people who are not benefitting or supporting you is to do it properly. You do not need to be rude or hurtful to them, you either need to tell them things are not working out, or just let yourselves grow apart naturally so you can form better relationships. How they react towards you is up to them, and you cannot control that, so all you need to do is wish them well, and hope that they do well in life no matter what. Who knows, maybe one day, your paths can cross again, and you can catch up like old friends from high school, but it all depends on how things end, how they react, and whether or not they move passed it and change for the better.

POSITIVE AND NEGATIVE ENERGY

I spent a lot of time in my life thinking that in order for life to be good, everything had to be positive and perfect. I realized later on that I was wrong, and that positive and negative need to balance each other out in order to keep us happy.

BALANCE

This does not mean that you want to have bad things in your life that hurt you, it simply means that if you only had positive in life, that kind of imbalance would make you unable to appreciate the good or fully understand when things are good. The secret to life is that we cannot always know and appreciate good things without understanding their opposites. In other words, you cannot know happiness without sadness, you cannot know pleasure without pain, and you cannot know light without darkness. When something is constant, we become numb to it, and it no longer phases us. When we have to struggle on some level or deal with some kind of stressor to get what we need, we get rewarded with good feelings.

Constantly having positive and negative counteract each other allows us to feel rewarded for overcoming a stressor. You can compare this type of balance to the magnetic poles of the earth. The positive and negative charges have to balance each other out in order to stabilize our planet and its orbit, just like positive and negative frequencies help keep us balanced as well. Struggles are meant to build us up to make us stronger and smarter, so we know how to survive and handle anything life throws at us. As time goes on, and we learn from our struggles, we handle situations better than we did before, and what once baffled us will now just brush off our shoulders like nothing.

MY FINAL THOUGHTS

Now, I know it may seem like our journey together is over, but this is only the beginning. My goal here was to offer you my support and wisdom to teach you what you need to know to start and get the ball rolling. Remember how I talked about motivation being like inertia in Chapter 10? Well, I hope that by reading my book, you have found your opposing force. It is now time to begin to build the life you wish to build to allow yourself to level up.

Chapter 17

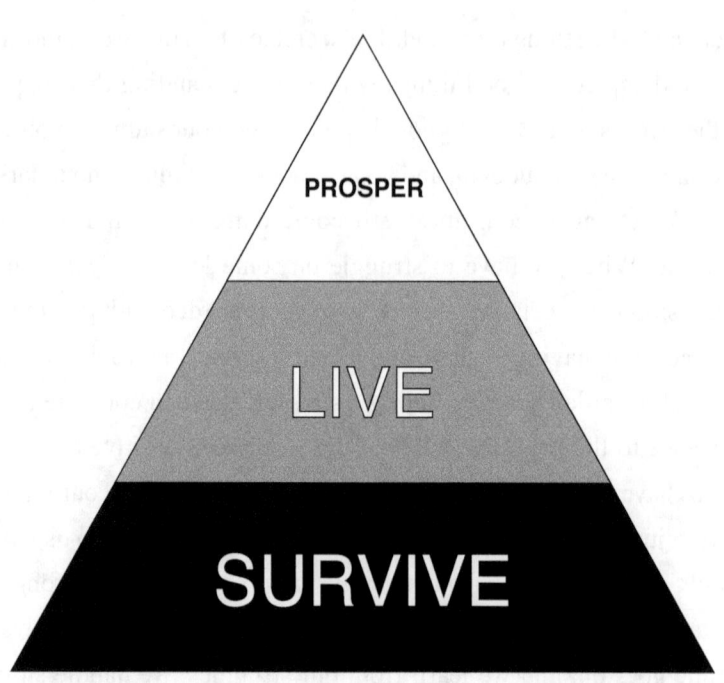

In life, there are three basic levels, surviving, living, and prospering. In order to get to the higher levels, you must conquer the lower ones. In other words, in order to prosper, you need to know how to live, and in order to live, you need to know how to survive. Surviving simply means staying alive biologically and getting by economically and financially, living involves actually being able to enjoy life and do many of the things you want to do with the ones you love, and prospering is when you become the very best version of yourself in all aspects of life.

We are all capable of prospering in our own ways. In order to become unlimited, we must remove the limits we set for ourselves. Once we do that, we can excel far greater than we ever could have imagined. So go out there, make positive changes in your life, figure out what you want, and go get it! I have faith in you, and I am here to support you the whole way. The time to start living your ideal life is now!

Acknowledgements

Thank you so much for reading my book, it really means the world to me. I hope you found it helpful in starting your journey with me to the life you want and deserve. It is crucial that you understand the importance of closure and showing appreciation by acknowledging all of the significant people in your life who have made a real impact in shaping who you are today, both the good and the bad. As an example, I would like to share this message with you and the following people; the ones I've hurt, the ones who've hurt me, the ones who've hurt me and I've hurt back, and the ones who've helped me:

"To those of you who've I hurt, I just want you to know that I am very truly sorry for all of the pain I've caused you. I was simply in a lot of pain myself and I projected it onto you. You did not deserve such harsh treatment, but I failed to be strong enough not to let my problems get the best of me. I hope someday you can find it in your heart to forgive me and understand where I come from.

To the ones who've hurt me, what you did affected me deeply, and I was in a dark place for many years because of it. After overcoming my demons, I have learned a lot. I now understand where you come from, the pain you've experienced in your life, and that you may not have meant to do what you did. I forgive all of you and I wish you nothing but the best in life.

To the ones who've hurt me and I've hurt back, at the time I thought you deserved my revenge, but now I understand that what I did was wrong. I beat you down after you've already been beaten down in life, and I made your situation worse than it already was. I apologize for my ignorance and lack of understanding. I promise to handle future situations with kindness and compassion.

Acknowledgements

And finally, to the ones who've helped me, if it weren't for you, I wouldn't be the person I am today. You've saved my life, made me smile, made me laugh, guided me through my journey, supported me, taught me great things, and allowed me to prosper in a way I never could've imagined. I love you all, and I could never have gotten to where I am today without you.

As for me, there is nowhere to go but up. I promise to use my experiences and wisdom to help others, benefit society, and someday save the world."

Please do yourselves a favor, and at some point along our journey, when the time is right and you're in a better place, share this message to everyone who's made an impact, good or bad, on your life. Whether you do it directly or indirectly, you never know how good it can truly make them feel. Thanks again for reading, now put the book away; we've got a long journey ahead of us!

Acknowledgements

Special Thanks To The Following People

Gerry Robert
Travon Taylor
Paul Oliver
Terrie Scott
Patrick Travis
Elizabeth Brico
Jacoby Woodard
Erick Holmberg
David Baumgartner
John Doherty
Terri J. Kerr
Donald Ficken
Arlene Travis
Adrian Townsend
Ryan Travis
Elizabeth Crystal
Bill McLeod
John Sawyer
Lorraine Barry
Linda King
Nancy Parsons

and to all of my family, friends, supporters, and followers...

I Could Not Have Done It Without You

About The Author

Jack Travis is a mental health advocate, an author, a modern day philosopher, and a millennial entrepreneur. He struggled with many life-long mental illnesses as a result of abuse and other traumatic experiences. With his journey he started through social media, his goal is to teach other people how to overcome their struggles and find happiness in life. Jack is working on becoming a motivational speaker, and he wishes to encourage others to join him on his journey because we are truly stronger together.

"I spent years living in a dark place with a negative outlook on life; I hated myself, and I did not feel worthy or like I mattered to anyone because of how I was treated by most people. It was as if my eyes were not only open to the bad, but also closed to the good. Once I started getting the help I needed, and making positive changes in my life, I was able to overcome my struggles. Going through the process of healing and recovery taught me a lot, and now my goal is to help others with what I've learned and what I've discovered. We're all limited to our own knowledge, so we must be willing to broaden our horizons, learn from credible sources, and discover happier and healthier ways of life than what we are used to. After all, the harder we fall, the higher we can rise." – Jack Travis

www.iamjacktravis.com

Paul Oliver Photography

Thank You For The Awesome Photoshoot!

Photo taken by: shootmedash

Photo taken by: Jim LaSala *Photo taken by: Craft Photography*

www.pauloliverphotography.com
978-604-5771
pauloliversphotos@gmail.com

www.ingramcontent.com/pod-product-compliance
Lightning Source LLC
LaVergne TN
LVHW051608070426
835507LV00021B/2835